JANET DAVIS

Sacred healing

MRIs, Marigolds, & Miracles

TWENTY THIRD *23rd*
PUBLICATIONS
www.23rdpublications.com

This book is dedicated to our son,
Bob, the hero of this story.

TWENTY-THIRD PUBLICATIONS
A Division of Bayard
One Montauk Avenue, Suite 200
New London, CT 06320
(860) 437-3012 or (800) 321-0411
www.23rdpublications.com

The Scripture passages contained herein are from the *New Revised Standard Version of the
Bible,* copyright ©1989, by the Division of Christian Education of the National Council of
Churches in the U.S.A. All rights reserved.

Cover image ©2010 Photos.com, a division of Getty Images. All rights reserved.

ISBN 978-1-58595-798-9
Library of Congress Catalog Card Number: 2010925839
Printed in the U.S.A.

Foreword

I remember when I first sensed there was a fuller experience of being alive than I was living. Until that time I'd been living life primarily in my mind and imagination—always thinking about things, but seldom present to what was actually before me. I'd created a narrative of a good and just world, and in this story life was predictable and made sense. There were rules. There was a clear way that things should be. This image of life was my unquestioned reality.

I never guessed there was a difference between my image of life and life itself until life intervened in my narrative when I was twenty-seven years old. Without warning my young husband and daughter were killed in an accident involving a drunk driver. I literally blinked my eyes and everything I knew was gone: dreams, hopes, and anchors—especially my story about what life should be. There was the life I'd planned, and the one that was now unfolding. It was a tremendous jolt. But alongside this great loss was a remarkable pressure not to turn away from the experience, no matter how difficult it was to go on. Something in me knew that this was my opportunity to stop imagining life, and finally meet it face to face.

In the pages that follow, Janet Davis describes the moment when her own picture of life was replaced by life itself. She learns that her son has a serious and potentially grave medical diagnosis, and she wants to deny those words, even as she makes plans to insure her son's care. She writes from the heart of the experience about the fear that rises up. Life never stops to ask her if she's willing or ready to bear these hard truths. There are no considerations.

"Maybe I need to come up with some new language," she writes, searching for a way to describe her sense of isolation and fright. Then, with vulnerability, humor, and a striking honesty, she sets out on this unbidden journey, entering the proverbial dark wood where the pilgrim encounters the things that cannot be changed, regardless of your deepest wishes and fervent prayers. Janet walks into the dark woods with hands outstretched, feeling her way forward. "Will someone please clarify the rules for me?" she asks. In that single sentence she gives voice to the powerlessness and sense of bewilderment that characterize the path.

Her first solace is found in the smallest detail: She continues to water the marigolds in her garden. The ordinary task becomes an anchor against all that is rapidly shifting. While the future remains stubbornly uncertain, watering marigolds is manageable. Her entries continue, encompassing many salient steps of the journey: the frightening sound of alarming medical options given to someone you love; the search for inner and outer equilibrium as the things you've counted on prove to be moveable; the complexity of life; and then the surprising and perplexing existence, simultaneously, of pain and grace.

Scott Peck begins *The Road Less Traveled* with the memorable words, "Life is difficult." Crises arise without warning, and we're left to cope as best we can. It's like being at sea while high waves batter a small craft that is your only refuge. You cling to the rudder and face the wind and spray. As Janet endures stormy seas she continues to write and pray and search for answers. One day she considers that "[perhaps] whatever comes my way is the flow of my life." That realization is her gold: Whatever lies ahead, my way is the life being held out to me...the only life there is.

In the pages that follow, Janet allows us to stay in the boat beside her as she rides the storm. These particular circumstances are hers, but sooner or later we all face our own rough seas. As Janet's illusion of control falls away, she begins to find new compass points. There is blessed calm and grace as she returns over and over again to sit for morning and evening prayer at a beloved monastery, comforted by the familiarity of the psalms and chants. The ancient verses are a reminder that we are all here so briefly—yet these fleeting hours have power and meaning.

In Thornton Wilder's play *Our Town*, a young woman who has died returns to earth to re-live just one ordinary day. Overcome by the beauty of life she finally asks, "Doesn't anyone see what they have while they still have it? We never even look at one another."

In sharing Janet's journey we are encouraged to look more closely at those whom we deeply love, and perhaps see them through a clearer lens. These are the very people who'll teach us necessary lessons about life's brief and precious beauty. These are the ones able to move us closer to life's deeper teachings.

Throughout the journey Janet welcomes us to become more aware of life's ordinary moments. Her words suggest that all the ingredients we need are on our path; it's a matter of seeing. In the end life asks us to let go of our terms for life, and simply meet what is. Following her example, we keep walking forward, day after day. We pray, and water the marigolds. We become frustrated, lose our focus…then regroup and begin again. We slip into the monastery and watch slants of light filter through stained glass. One day life will hopefully succeed in breaking through in us. Then a door we never noticed opens wide.

ॐ૮ Paula D'Arcy

Preface

Crisis and loss come in many forms: death of a loved one, illness of a child, divorce, financial ruin, relational betrayal, diagnosis of cancer, incarceration, a car accident, sexual abuse, job loss, chronic disease, lawsuit... to name a few. In the midst of such painful moments, we tend to conclude that the love of God has vanished from our lives.

Yet, oddly, in one such season, I found the opposite to be true. When our oldest child and only son was diagnosed with an inoperable brain tumor several years ago, I found myself experiencing God's love in myriad new ways. Within the text of this book I offer you the details of that journey: some funny, some sad, some wise, some just plain ugly, and some full of beauty.

The kind of healing offered within these pages is not based on platitudes or easy answers. Instead it is a healing that trusts daring authenticity and the unseen yet sacred healing rhythms God has built into our souls. My prayer is that somewhere in the midst of these stories of MRIs and marigolds, you will glimpse your own experience of pain and loss and for some brief moment, not feel so alone. My confident hope is that in that moment of honesty and connection abides the gentle, healing presence of God.

Acknowledgements

Special thanks to...

My husband, Robert, my companion on this journey, who loves me as I am and gives me wings to fly.

To our daughters, Jenna and Betsy, who bless my life with their beauty, presence, and wisdom.

To the brothers of Holy Cross Monastery, Beaumont, Texas, whose kindness, wisdom, and generous hospitality shaped this journey and changed me forever.

To Tracie, whose sincere engagement of these words and generosity of heart revealed to me their healing power.

To Christie, whose encouragement and vision for this manuscript sustained my perseverance.

To the members of St. Stephen's, Beaumont. You are God's face and embrace to me.

To our family and friends who helped us on this journey. Though many of your good deeds are mentioned in this work, many more are not. Thank you all. Your kindness will not be forgotten, by us or by God.

To Paul Pennick and the editorial staff of Twenty-Third Publications who understood and dared to believe the notion that an authentic story can be more healing than answers.

Can you top this?

At the end of this last summer, I was at a wedding reception visiting with a friend's son, Andrew. I was excited to discover that he had just graduated from the same law school our son, Bob, was to begin the following Monday. He told me all about his first day.

"I had a ninety-minute drive and left in plenty of time until I realized thirty minutes out that I had left my briefcase with all the briefs I had prepared for class. It was the worst day. I sweated out every minute of class, hoping no one would call on me. I sure hope Bob's first day is better than mine."

"I'm sure he'll do fine." I was comfortable and confident inside and out. "After all," I thought, "he's gotten himself into law school (no small feat), arranged for the money to pay for it, and found a place to live. What could go wrong now?"

About noon of Bob's first day, the phone rang. "Mom, Dr. Ramon's office just called. They said some of my lab work was off and they want me to have an MRI. They think there might be something wrong with my brain."

The mom in me was calm, reassuring him and telling him I would handle the details and let him know when and where. The former nurse in me was frantic.

That nurse part of me had insisted on a check-up before Bob started law school. It was the prudent thing to do every four years or so, no matter how well you were feeling. It was also the nurse part of me who knew this doctor well enough to know that he would never order a pricey test like an MRI without a very good reason.

We scheduled the test for Friday.

Next time I see Andrew, I imagine the conversation will begin something like, "Can you top this?"

► Can you recall the first moment when you had some sense that trouble or loss might be headed your way?

God, as I begin this journey of remembering my pain and loss, grant me strength for the journey.

❧ One drop at a time

For several years now, I have worked as a hospital chaplain, first full time, then part time, and now relief. One of the bits of wisdom I encountered along the way was a new definition for a common stage of the grieving process: denial. An experienced hospice worker once told me, "My definition of denial is 'absorbing things a drop at a time.' Sometimes that's the only way hard truths can be absorbed."

We got the results of Bob's MRI the next Monday. Our son had a brain tumor in the center of his head, near his pituitary gland. The tumor was 2.9cm x 1.4cm x 1.5cm, about the size of an unshelled peanut.

"So what does that mean? What's next?" I asked the doctor.

"Well, we'll try to get him in to some specialists in Houston as soon as possible. And we're going to run more tests while we wait." That's all I heard that day…not because it was all that was said, but it was all I *could* hear.

Later, as unwelcome realities continued to persistently unfold, I recalled that there were other things said that day like, "Well, it may not be an ordinary pituitary tumor." And, "I think he should go ahead and withdraw for the semester." I just wasn't ready to hear what I wasn't ready to hear.

So, we began to research pituitary tumors. The news was not all bad… in fact, technically speaking, they weren't even considered to be brain tumors. Most can be removed with endoscopic surgery, with little more than an overnight stay in the hospital. It seemed doable. Hey, we can handle this one.

Later that week, as we prepared for the additional tests, I collected Bob's films and the report from the initial MRI. I pored over the computer. Neurosurgery was not my field of expertise, never mind the fact that I had not practiced nursing for almost twenty years! Oddly, the terms were different than those in the pituitary tumor information I had been researching…an observation I made on some level and completely ignored in every other way. One drop at a time, just one drop at a time.

▶ Reflect on your own process of absorbing new, frightening, or painful realities "one drop at a time."

God of all compassion, grant me patience with myself and those in my world who simply need more time.

❧ So this is the abundant life?

Many years ago, when our two girls were ages three weeks and three years and Bob was six years old, our family took a long car trip from Texas to Minnesota. (Yes, I said three weeks old…but that's a whole other story). One of the kids' favorite things on that trip was to listen to a cassette tape by a Christian comedian, Mark Lowry. About the twelfth time through, I began to realize that he was not only funny, he was also wise.

He pointed out that we usually interpret Jesus' words about abundant life as if He were promising us a good time, all the time. *Life* is not always a good time; instead, it is like a roller coaster, with high and low points. To live the abundant life meant to live fully present to it all, the highest highs and the lowest lows. Adopting that definition in theory turned out to be a whole lot easier than living it in reality.

The same day we found out Bob did indeed have a tumor was also the day I signed my first book contract, a very big deal for a first-time author. Life was getting just a bit too abundant for my taste. In fact, I felt quite crazy. How in the world could I order all this emotion? How could I celebrate? How could I *not* celebrate? I was all over the map!

Of course, if I could—if life worked that way—I would give back the contract if I could also give back my son's tumor. Bargaining: another stage of grief. Life just doesn't work that way.

Left in the chaos of all my emotions, I began to notice that trying to order them was of no use whatsoever. My best option, perhaps my only real option, was just to feel them, to agree to be wherever I was at any given moment. Authenticity became my gathering point, the place where all things fell together rather than apart, the location of my sanity.

I began to surrender my need to prescribe or conjure or explain a way to cope with my life as it was, and became more concerned with accurately describing it in the moment, whatever that moment might hold. Rather than controlling my life (hopeless!), I wanted to learn to engage it and *live* it…the good, the bad, and the ugly. So, this is the abundant life.

▶ Spend ten minutes free-writing your thoughts and feelings: the good, the bad, and the ugly. Dare to believe that authentically living what you feel is a more healing path than trying to shape your internal responses into a prescribed, acceptable, tidy or comfortable form.

God, you may not be afraid of my feelings, but sometimes I am. Courage, God, I want courage to live this journey through.

✖✦ Free fall

The best description I can offer of our first few encounters with specialists is that of a free fall. Though I have never leapt from an airplane or dared to bungee jump, I have experienced such a rapid onset of disappointment that my stomach felt as if it rose into my throat.

Our first appointment was with a neuro-ophthalmologist, Dr. Stedman. She was a kind and curious soul, and the first thing she did was to pop Bob's MRI films on the viewing box and begin to "ooh" and "ahh." The second thing she did was to call her partner and all available students into the room and proceed to explain to them that this was *not* a pituitary tumor.

"Ping" went my eyelids, springing open. "Thud" went my stomach. I suddenly remembered what I had chosen to forget about the MRI report. There had been no mention of a pituitary tumor. So, what was this?

No one there seemed to know. What was clear from the tone of conversation was that this was going to be significantly more complicated than we had originally thought. All they could determine after a full seven hours of testing was that whatever it was had miraculously spared Bob's vision for now. Though the tumor was touching the optic nerve on three sides and shifting one of his optic tracts, his vision remained unimpaired. Not even my gratitude for such grace removed the heaviness in my gut.

The free fall continued with our first visit to a neurosurgeon. In spite of our experience with Dr. Stedman, we were still hoping to hear that this tumor would qualify for the "quick fix." After all, she was not a neurosurgeon.

I knew the news was not good when Dr. Robbins prefaced his remarks with recognition that we had just met him and had little personal reason to trust his judgment. "Ping" went my eyelids. "Thud" went my stomach.

He went on to say that he did not believe the tumor was operable. It was centered above the pituitary, integrally entwined with exquisitely sensitive endocrine structures in addition to the optic nerve, and surgery could do more harm than good. He recommended biopsy alone. Unfortunately, even that diagnostic procedure would require a mini-craniotomy, shaved head and all. Is there any such thing as a *mini*-craniotomy?

Will this brick in my stomach ever go away? When will we reach the bottom of the bad news? When will we reach the end of this free fall?

▶ Have you had "free fall" moments in your journey, moments when the depths of your pain and loss were increasing with every breath?

Save me, O God.

❧ When words won't come

As you might imagine, as this story began to intrude into our lives, prayer was a large part of our response. One evening in particular, when anxiety was high and comfort low, my husband asked me to spend some time in prayer with him.

His request was reasonable. For decades, we had prayed together about the various concerns that life had brought our way. In fact, years ago we had hosted a small group of fellow church members for a weekly prayer meeting in our home, repeatedly asking God to bless the small Bible church we were attending at the time. Conversational prayer had been a part of our lives for a long time.

But, for me, in that moment, on that particular evening, the words simply would not come. The openness in my heart and my deeply felt inclination toward God were definitely present, they simply could not be expressed, or perhaps better said, contained by words.

Though my silence was unsettling for my husband, I was more intrigued than upset. There was a real sense of freedom and a deeply seated peace as I let go of words. My longing, fully and authentically experienced in the presence of God more than expressed to God, was enough. For the first time I knew that prayer of supplication happens even when words do not come.

A few days later, I went shopping for a pendant necklace in celebration of my book contract. I enjoy celebrating such milestones in a sacramental way, connecting them to something ordinary that can become a physical part of my life, a concrete reminder of God's faithfulness to me. Months before, some Venetian glass pendant necklaces had caught my eye and seemed like just the thing.

The one I chose was a large aquamarine-colored glass bead with a beautifully reflective silver core. Interestingly, it was about the size and shape of our son's tumor. Ahh, a point of intersection in this crazy, abundant life of mine. Only this dual symbol could contain all that was in my heart. That glass bead became my prayer…an image of both the celebration of, and the longing for, beauty even when it comes in the unlikely shape of a tumor.

Prayer happens. Prayer cannot help but happen. Prayer is within and all around me, even when words won't come.

▸ Is your approach to connecting with God changing in the midst of this difficult season? What is working? What is not?

"Your face, Lord, do I seek." Psalms 27:8b

Caught by the rhythm of life

I wasn't prepared to get that kind of a phone call that morning. I had gone to San Antonio on a short business trip with my husband. On the medical front, we were waiting to hear about appointment dates to see other specialists and get a second opinion from another neurosurgeon. I was looking forward to some time away to work on my book. I was hopeful that perhaps a different setting would allow me to leave behind some of the grief, pain, and fear of home.

Bob called just before noon, utterly distraught. My easygoing son had hit a wall. He said he could not even decide whether to go to class that afternoon or not. He was completely overwhelmed, utterly paralyzed.

Though it was tempting to become the mom who simply took it from there, took over all decision-making capacity, ordering his world with specific direction, something within warned me of the danger of assuming that course with this twenty-three-year-old man who happened to be my son.

Instead of making decisions for him, I encouraged him to take the next thirty minutes to journal in a non-stop, stream of consciousness kind of way and see what decision floated to the top. He was to call back in an hour.

Thankfully, God brought clarity. At least for now, Bob needed a break. Though he had been able to keep up with his law school homework through these four weeks, a very significant accomplishment, everything else in life had become undoable: laundry, meals, even keeping up his apartment. There was no space or place for the ordinary rhythm of life.

As we spoke, I began to recognize the importance of that rhythm for me. It had been those ordinary tasks of groceries and laundry that had kept me moving forward during this time of great internal challenge and chaos. As I listened to the pain of his heart and his disorientation, I began to imagine how the lack of that kind of rhythm in his life had perhaps multiplied the anguish of this experience. A path of healing began to take shape.

He called it "mom's rhythm therapy." Having made the decision to take this week off before making a decision about continuing this semester of law school, the focus became sleeping and eating, cooking and cleaning, resting and exercising. We both learned the healing power of the ordinary. In our current state of free fall, we were both blessedly caught by the rhythm of life.

▶ Are you finding comfort in any moments of ordinary experience? Tasks, smells, places, relationships, touch, hobbies, tastes?

Open my heart, God, to experiences of comfort from both unexpected and utterly ordinary places. I need all I can get.

✿ Making room for grief

Bob's tumor, affectionately known as "Mr. Peanut" (No offense intended toward the *real* Mr. Peanut—yum!), entered my life as a very unwelcome guest, an intruder, a stranger. And he brought his equally unwelcome friends: grief and pain. I knew these guests were here to stay for a while. Even if this ordeal resulted in complete wholeness for our son, the reality of the traumatic experience of it all was a genuine loss. As much as I disliked the thought, I realized early on that a large part of coping well in this moment hinged upon the choice to make room in my life for these unexpected and unwanted visitors.

Finding a place for Bob's tumor was pretty straightforward. Research and doctor appointments, dealing with insurance and medical bills took blocks of focused time. But his friends—pain and grief—were not so predictable. How much time do I set aside to support my son? How could I know or predict in any way when or where or how his needs would surface?

And how do you make room in your life for grief? It surfaces at unprescribed times in erratic ways. It is fickle at best. How much time will it take to mourn a loss whose depth I do not yet know? How do you make room in your life for grief?

I am sure the answer to that question is as varied as the prints on the tips of all our fingers. For me, it meant offloading what I could from my schedule, declining new invitations for involvement, and making myself available to myself as well as to my son.

You see, my biggest challenge in hard times is self-awareness. When I am in pain, I struggle to remain connected to what I am feeling because, let's face it, feeling pain is no fun. Busyness is by far the most convenient anesthetic of the soul for most Americans. If I do not know where or who I am in this moment, how can I possibly be available to help my son?

So, I bought new watercolor paper for daily quiet, creative self-expression. I declined a committee appointment at church. I brought my journal out again. And I made a point of attending Morning, Noon, or Evening Prayer at a local monastery more often.

When pain and grief surfaced, I became intentional about *not* running in the other direction. There is no healing in running. I began to make peace with these unwelcome guests, learning the wise and subtle art of making room for grief.

▶ How has the pace of your life changed in this season of hard times? Though making room to experience grief often feels impossible, the reality is that carrying it is even worse.

Grant me grace, God, to somehow find a way to welcome this stranger.

You know your adult son has moved home when…

You know your adult son has moved home when…

Your TV is suddenly hooked up to a woofer.

Your fine china has been moved to the cupboard, replaced by a variety of pub glasses.

The family now has to play by all the official Scrabble rules including challenges (You will recall that he is a law student.).

Steak and dark beer appear weekly on your grocery list.

Your older daughter's bedroom has been turned into one giant bed as he adjoins rather than replaces the twin with his full-size bed.

You make an appointment with your veterinarian to sort through a disagreement among your children as to whether a new pug puppy would be a positive or negative addition to your family, which already includes a sixteen-year-old dachshund named Frank.

Homemade Guinness ice cream occupies a quarter of your freezer space.

A lime green and white rug with the word "RELAX" appears in your hallway.

The upstairs bedroom has become extra attic space.

You have yet another pair of shoes left on the floor of your bedroom at the end of the day.

Your pantry stock items now include Life cereal.

After we finally acknowledged to ourselves the complex realities of this tumor, Bob made the decision to defer his law school admission until the next fall, withdrew from school, and moved home (a full six weeks after our family doctor had first recommended that course). And thus began our list of "You know your adult son has moved home when…."

▶ What physical or environmental changes have entered your world? Have any of them brought laughter or even joy?

God, open my heart to change of all kinds and sorts and to sparks of joy even in the midst of pain and fear.

✿ Maintaining marigolds

Years ago I noticed that when I am stressed, I forget to water my plants. Actually, it isn't that I forget, because I do tend to notice that they are dry, wilting, in need (sometimes *desperate* need) of my care. Yet, for whatever reason, I do not have the capacity to care for them. I cannot seem to focus long enough to actually give them what they need. I remember even wondering to myself, "Why in the world don't you just water them? It would lower your stress level!"

Though I don't really have an answer to that pretty obvious question, I did observe the other day that, at least for now, in the midst of this significant life crisis, my marigolds are getting watered. That is a particularly impressive data point because they are in southern-facing window boxes and require daily attention to survive.

Knowing that this difference was not due to some disciplined determination to not let my gardening prowess suffer on this tumor journey, I began to wonder about what was different within me this time that somehow allowed me to still tend to these tender plants.

Again, I am not sure I really have an answer to that question either, but I do have an observation. I think it has something to do with being less distracted. Think about that word: dis-traction, "apart" from traction, without traction.

I have lived through most of the hard times in my life in a state of "spinning." Hyper-alert and frightened, I take in huge amounts of information, yet I am too disconnected from the rest of myself to actually do much about whatever it is I see. Noticing but not watering the plants is undoubtedly just the tip of the iceberg. I cringe to think of how my children's needs have not been met during these seasons of challenge.

Though I could speculate about this difference within, ultimately all speculation would end at the same place: grace. Whether it is the plethora of prayers offered by friends, family, and even strangers on our behalf or the result of healthier choices or simply being forty-seven years old, my experience of greater peace and freedom is sheer grace, celebrated in this particular moment as maintaining marigolds.

▶ What are your external signs of stress? Dead plants, weight loss, isolation, clutter? What are your internal signs? Anger? Confusion? Deadness? How do you find yourself today?

I give thanks for the grace of this day, wherever it may find me on this journey.

❧ Coping conflicts

We were just turning out of the parking garage at M.D. Anderson Hospital in the midst of the towering Texas Medical Center in Houston. Perhaps it was the stark transition from the shady garage into the still hot September sun, but as we turned that corner, something woke up inside of me. I suddenly realized that we were in the midst of our first coping conflict.

Married for twenty-five years this last June, my husband and I have learned a few things about one another through the years. Some of the most helpful insights have come from personality-analysis information. I am an introvert. He is an extrovert.

We had just finished meeting with Dr. Parsons, the second neurosurgeon, for our first of what turned out to be many "second" opinions. The problem with second opinions is that when you ask for one, you just might get one. In other words, there was part of us that wanted to hear the same thing the first doctor said. Even though we did not particularly like the news he gave us, at least that would have removed any ambiguity or decision-making burden.

Unlike Dr. Robbins, Dr. Parsons felt Bob's brain tumor was operable, or at least possibly operable and worth an attempt. Rather than recommending a mini-craniotomy for biopsy only, he preferred a full craniotomy with the goal of complete cure through total resection (removal). We are talking ten-plus hours of surgery with an ear-to-ear incision, removal of the front of the skull, etc. Not to mention a possible two months of recovery, fifty-percent-plus chance of increased endocrine dysfunction, and a five-to-ten percent chance of blindness. *Big* risks. *Big* potential rewards. A lot to think about.

As an introvert, when I receive a boatload of new information, especially such weighty information, I immediately respond by turning inward. I am not shut down as much as focused within. I need space, silence, and time alone to process all I have heard and regain a sense of personal stability.

As an extrovert, my husband needs to talk. He processes things conversationally, outside of himself. Can you see it coming?

I wish I could say that astute observation and understanding were enough to resolve coping conflicts.

▶ How do you best process new or frightening information? What do those around you need?

God, we are doing the best that we can.

❧ For what shall I ask?

"Ask and you shall receive that your joy may be full."

I heard that verse again the other day and it created quite a dilemma within me. I don't know what to ask for.

When Bob was fifteen years old and taking driver's education, I dropped him off one day at a nearby strip mall for his driving instruction class. This was the students' second day of actually being behind the wheel of a real live car. Needless to say, this faithful mom said a prayer for his safety as I was driving off.

Though I did not actually hear words, I nonetheless heard a voice say, "What if being safe isn't the best thing for him?" Ugh. What do I do with that? Inside I thought, "Okay, whatever."

Sure enough, that day he had an accident. Thankfully, it was a mere fender bender, the other driver's fault, and an experience that took a small bit of the "invincible teen" edge off his attitude toward this new privilege.

Ever since that day, though, I have a hard time knowing how to pray. That story surfaces every time I want to pray for safety…for my children, myself, or others. I have heard it said that God is good, but God is not safe. My experience in life and my reading of Scripture seems to agree with that insight.

Now, let's be clear: I do not believe God shames me in any way for praying for safety. It is definitely not "wrong." But, I often feel invited by God to stretch my definition of goodness, to not limit my view of goodness to only those things in life that are safe. To be willing to trust more in God's faithfulness to redeem a loss than in my desire to avoid all loss. God invites me in large and small ways to act out the truth that heaven really is greater than Eden.

So, do I pray for the tumor to disappear? For all the endocrine structures to be shielded during surgery? For the optic nerve to be protected? Or do I pray for the strength to bear the burden of medically controlled endocrine insufficiency for the rest of his life? Or the willingness to accept blindness and live well in the midst of it? For what shall I ask?

▶ What do you want from God in this moment? Think boldly and broadly.

God, you said, "Ask," so here you go...

Deeper still

A friend of mine was doing a beach retreat a few weekends ago and invited me to join her. Having spent the better part of the previous two days visiting with doctors, I needed a break.

The morning after I arrived, I did not pick up my prayer necklace to put it on. A part of me felt guilty, like I was abandoning my son in some way. But a stronger voice within, trained by years of hospital chaplaincy, knew the healthy wisdom of that choice. The tumor was not in my brain; it was in my son's. It was good to remember that reality and free myself, on occasion, from carrying that load.

Since I was one of the first to waken, I took my Bible and watercolors out onto the large deck. In my pajamas, I sat in silence. I turned my face into the steady breeze. It comforted and refreshed me as it blew through my hair. I listened to the loud and rhythmic waves, crashing time and time and time again against the shore. I felt the sting of tears in my eyes and just let them fall and fall and fall over my eyelids, down my cheeks, beyond my neck, into my heart.

This was intended to be the weekend my husband and I would be spending in England. It was a trip we had thoughtfully planned and struggled to save for. It was our wild celebration of twenty-five years of marriage. It had been a deep-seated and long-standing dream of my heart. It was a great loss to my soul. *My* soul. Suddenly, I realized just why I needed to set aside that necklace today. Today, the tears were for *me*.

I cried and hurt and grieved. At one point I opened my Bible to Psalm 95:4 that we sing in church: "In his hands are the depths of the earth." The depths. It felt as if my soul was exploring the depths of disappointment that day. It wasn't just the trip, it was what the trip symbolized: all my long-standing, deeply seated dreams.

Would there ever be room in life for them? Would there ever be room in my life for me? The oddest thing was that I knew only I could answer that question. It had been me, and no one else, who had made the decision to give up this trip to be with our son. I did not regret that choice.

That day, I simply bore the pain of disappointment and unanswerable questions, plunging into the depths, reminded by the wind and the waves and the Word that God's hands and God's love are deeper still.

▶ What has your deepest point of personal pain been thus far? Try to make that simple observation without needing to judge or explain or even understand your experience of pain.

God, today I need to know, to feel, that your hands go deeper still than my pain. Hold me.

❧ Grief is an antidote for fear

Have you ever had a really profound insight pop into your head at a really odd moment? Well, that's what happened to me not long ago as I was standing in line at the credit union. I suddenly realized that grief is an antidote for fear.

Let me start at the beginning. The subject of grief has been an inexplicable theme in my life for a long time. In nursing school, I took an elective course on death and dying. When I went to graduate school, the particular program I chose had an emphasis on grief as a part of the process of change. Even my favorite theologian, Walter Brueggemann, writes often about the biblical theme of grief as a critically important part of God's work in this world. I led grief groups for my church. And when I went back to work after being home for twenty years, I took a job as a hospital chaplain.

Grief is also somehow connected to my spiritual giftedness. I call myself a "grief magnet." For some reason, in my presence, many people feel especially comfortable to let their grief surface. Maybe it's because I have such a vision for the goodness of the grief process.

From my years of experience as a chaplain, Bible student, and reflective person, I have become convinced that, in the course of life, we all encounter pain and loss of some sort. Though grief is the natural, human response to those experiences, interestingly, most of us see grief as something that diminishes us. We use expressions like, "I'm going to melt into a puddle of tears" or we say, "I can't fall apart now." Think about those images…they connect the act of grieving with a diminishing of personhood.

Ironically, I have observed repeatedly that it is not grief that diminishes us, but rather the avoidance of grief that can eat away at our souls. Grief is an organic response to loss. In refusing to grieve, we are forestalling a very natural healing process and disconnecting ourselves from our deepest personal reality: We become less than who we truly are.

If, on the other hand, we engage this natural healing process, somehow, counter-intuitively, the pain and loss become building blocks for new strength. And, if through the process of grieving, pain and loss can become our friends, is there anything in this world we need to fear? So, in line at the credit union one day, I concluded: Grief is an antidote for fear.

▶ How do you tend to think about grief? As a healing process or a necessary evil? As something imposed upon you or as something you choose? As helpful or inherently harmful? As making you weak or strong?

Wisdom is nice, God. Such a vision is lovely. But this stuff still hurts. God. It still hurts.

❦ Oh, but you are helping

"If only I could do something to help!" my friends say to me.
Oh, but you are helping. This is what help looks like.

An invitation to the beach.

A meal for the kids when I am out of town.

Letting me leave in tears.

Letting me stay in tears.

A promise to pray.

A gift of Snickerdoodles.

A hand-tied University of Texas blanket.

A challenging but flexible job at a law firm.

Reading an X-ray at 7 AM.

Affirming my decision to decline a church committee appointment.

A knowing hug.

Two sisters holding a prayer service in their living room for our son.

An elderly woman's donation to M.D. Anderson Hospital.

A gift of English beer and a book on the Trinity.

Your tears.

An invitation to lunch.

The steady rhythm of Evening Prayer.

Oh, but you are helping.

▶ Has help come to you this week? From friends or strangers? What has it looked like?

Thanks, God, for amazing friends. How I need their love right now. Somehow, keep me connected, keep me honest and open.

Reshaped bodies, re-formed souls

It is an odd thought that this tumor might have been in our son's head since birth. They tell us that is almost certainly the case. It has always been a part of him. His design from the beginning. What an odd thought.

Does that make the tumor normal for him, his unique normal? Or is it imperfection? Does the fact that it is now disrupting other hormones change it from normal to an imperfection?

Just knowing the tumor is there has forced a change in how we see Bob's body. He used to be well, now he's sick. He used to be normal. Now he's not.

It seems like one of the most painful aspects of illness is the fact that when our bodies are reshaped—or even discovered to be a different shape than we knew them to be—something new is required of our souls.

I ponder what his life would be like if the five-to-ten percent chance of post-surgical blindness becomes a reality for him. Certainly, he *could* adapt. He is smart and has good support.

But *would* he adapt? Would he allow his reshaped body to re-form his soul in such a way that he could live as a whole person in the midst of blindness?

There. I'll say it. My deepest fear is not blindness but bitterness. The blindness we could help him live with. The bitterness would be slow suicide, a protracted process of soul death. I don't know if I could bear to watch that.

I have a friend who is struggling to age with grace. For years, as arthritis has brought pain and new limitations into her life, her soul has been unable or unwilling to re-form. She has become more and more reclusive and angry. Anxiety and sleep disturbances are now common, and depression is beginning to take hold.

So, what is health? What is wholeness? Is it a state of the body? Conformity to some standard of physical perfection? Or is it a condition of the soul? Surrender to the inevitable reality of reshaped bodies, re-formed souls?

▶ Has the crisis in your life changed your understanding of health or wholeness? Has it changed your body or that of someone you love? If so, how? What is your deepest fear in this new life reality?

God, sometimes it feels as if too many things are changing all at once. The waters of my mind and heart are muddy. I stand before you now, muddy and still, hopeful that the mud will sink.

Words I never wanted to hear

The supper table at our house is a sacred space. Good food. Good conversation. Good memories. Through the years, we have fought hard to preserve this tradition in spite of the pull of external pressures like extracurricular school activities, church committee meetings, and demanding careers. We have also defended the time against the internal pressures of teens who (justifiably) felt that eating with their family was a part of their life they needed to hide from peers for the sake of avoiding ridicule.

As this tumor journey inserted itself into our lives, Bob was living in Houston, two hours from home and three hours from all the friends he had left behind from undergraduate school in Austin. He knew no one in Houston. So, several times a week, we drove to Houston for a nice dinner out. Though costly in terms of time and money, those gatherings were an essential part of coping for all of us. Interestingly, I never made the connection between that choice and our family history until a wise and observant friend, Madison, pointed it out to me.

After Bob moved home, our table times continued. As I described before, part of Bob's "rhythm therapy" was learning to cook, a skill he had somehow avoided acquiring in all his years at home. His creative culinary contributions made the times together even more interesting.

At one such meal, as we were casually conversing about our day, he said, "I want you all to know that I definitely want to be an organ donor.

I mean, if the worst happens, make sure they use my organs. And if I'm not going to wake up, take me off the machines."

I took a deep breath and our conversation continued as if those words had been a natural part of dinner-table talk.

In the days since that moment, I have come to recognize the significance of those words more and more. It had been too much to "unpack" then and there. The chaplain in me knows just how much raw courage it took on his part to say those words. They are *never* lightly spoken. I am proud beyond belief to have a son with such courage in such an impossibly difficult moment in his young life.

At the same time, the mom in me knows that those are words I never wanted to hear.

▶ Have there been any moments of heart-stopping conversation in your journey? When things were spoken that you never wanted to hear?

O, God, with your help, may my soul receive even those hard things I never wanted to hear.

❧ The decision is yours

"The decision is yours." I must have said those words to my son a hundred times over the last several weeks. Not because *he* needed to hear it, but because I did.

You see, he is twenty-three. He is an adult. But just barely. There is still a lot of that teenage invincibility going on inside him. He still exudes that youthful glowing optimism and innocence that none of us could have survived those years without. He does not pay his cell phone bill or car insurance yet. I am not even sure he knows how to balance a checkbook. He has no idea what a health insurance explanation of benefits even looks like.

And these decisions are *big* decisions. Does he opt to wait until symptoms force him into surgery, doing serial MRIs to watch whatever this thing is, hopeful he can catch it before a crisis, before it becomes more difficult to remove? Or does he go after it, accepting the fifty-percent-plus risk of losing all pituitary function and being dependent on medicines for the rest of his life? Not to mention the five-to-ten percent chance of permanent visual damage or blindness? *Big* decisions.

"The decision is yours." He has to make it as a twenty-three-year-old. He is not a forty-seven-year-old, so he cannot make it as one. He can listen to me, but he cannot be me. *He* will have to bear this decision, 24/7. *He* will have to live out any consequences for good or for ill.

Amazingly, he is not running from making the decision. When we meet with doctors, he engages them with questions as much as or more than we do. He knows this is his decision and has accepted that burden. He seems to have a strong awareness of God's help in the midst of all this. He is so courageous.

I am trying to be the mother of an adult child. I somehow was not prepared for the fact that even as you lose control of decisions and the ability to direct or protect their lives, you don't in *any* way lose the love and concern. You don't in any way lose the love and concern even as you say over and over again, "The decision is yours."

▶ Reflect for a moment on the decisions being made in the midst of your unfolding painful situation. Are they all yours? Others? A mix? Are you avoiding making decisions that are yours to make? Or are you seeking to control decisions that are not yours?

God, you are the Source of wisdom. Give it abundantly to all concerned here.

❧ A Gen X Psalm

Have you ever read the lament of a godly person from Generation X? Well, I could show you one, but I wouldn't dare because the amount of profanity just might offend you so much that you would miss the message.

Our son, Bob, the hero of this story, wrote one the other day. We had just come from our first meeting with the endocrinologist. More than any of the doctors we had met thus far, this kind man was able to give us the most likely "this is what you will be living with long term" scenario. Though he did not seem unrealistic, he did make it sound doable. I am not sure why that meeting had such a healing, freeing impact. Maybe it is because it spoke to a future beyond this fearful surgery piece. For whatever reason, we left there more hopeful and less anxious.

A part of that release was felt and expressed by Bob in the sudden realization that he had communicated very little with his friends through the ordeal of the last several weeks. (You mean it hasn't been *years*?!) For Bob, who greatly values his friends, that kind of silence was very unusual.

As soon as we got home, he sat down at the computer and set to work. He brought the calendar into his room and asked questions about dates of important events so he could be accurate. But this was no ordinary recounting of the facts. A bright mind with a very, very good sense of humor, he regaled his friends with such a tale. It was so very good to see his wild, edgy, creative streak re-emerging.

As I noted above, he felt free to use less than lovely language to entertain, shock, and even offend his readers, in part allowing them to experience a bit of this offensive intrusion that now abided in his brain.

As a chaplain accustomed to actually celebrating such honest expression, I took the language in stride. However, Robert, my husband, struggled an entire weekend with a deeply offended sense of morality and concern for our son's spiritual well-being. Wisely seeking help processing his own response, he got Bob's permission to share his composition with our pastor.

Logan, our pastor, listened well to my husband's concerns. He heard his fears. He confessed that he, too, might have written such a piece at twenty-three. He also helped my husband see what a rare gift this letter was for us: a sacred glimpse into Bob's vulnerable, internal experience of this horrific ordeal. He labeled it the noble work of a godly man. He called it a Gen X Psalm.

▶ How honest have you been with your friends? With God? Does the way you express yourself reflect your struggle or seek to negate or undo the honest expression of your current reality?

Thanks, God, for your ever compassionate listening ear.

✦ Enough

My soul is inflamed today. My heart is aching and raging.

"ENOUGH!"

Our older daughter, Jenna, called last night from her university to tell us that the routine X-ray she had done this week for a TB screening test in preparation for a study-abroad program showed a possible problem.

A problem? As if we don't have enough problems right now.

ENOUGH!

We made arrangements for a visit with her doctor here, settled on transportation plans, and began to collect past X-rays that would hopefully resolve this dilemma without further expense.

ENOUGH!

It's probably just a variation on normal. A repeat chest X-ray will resolve it.

ENOUGH!

But what if it is something serious? Or what if she just needs a CAT scan to get the form signed? Even with insurance, how will we possibly afford the $800 co-pay?

ENOUGH!

She so wants to go to Africa.

My daily watercolor is filled with fragmented pinks and reds.

My soul is inflamed. Sore. Hurting. Tender. Aching.

ENOUGH!

Suddenly I realize that even here, God meets me. Not in serene blues and greens that would shame my pain and rage. God meets me in red-hot compassion. God engages, enters, and joins my pain and rage.

ENOUGH! Will you be enough?

► Have you had "enough" yet?

Enough! Do you hear me, God!...Do you hear me, God?

🌿 In search

I've learned a lot from my monk friend, John. With a common interest in spiritual direction, we talk about all sorts of things. Some of my favorite conversations are around observations we share regarding various personality types. We reflect on what inspires some people and leaves others unmoved. Or how spiritual growth varies from one type to another. We also talk about what things in life move us toward freedom and when we notice ourselves caught in compulsive behaviors, going around in circles, not aware of what it is we are really seeking.

Since Bob's tumor entered our lives, I have done a lot of Internet research: from online medical dictionaries to physician credentials to familiarizing myself with neurosurgery institutes around the country to preferred provider lists for our insurance plan. The hours at the computer have really added up.

Several weeks into this journey, we had sufficient information to formulate a basic plan of attack. It would take several more weeks for it to all play out due to shipping films here and there and waiting for doctors to return from vacations.

As I waited, I found myself doing more Internet research. More. And more. And more. Following ridiculously slim leads that never ended up with information or resources half as good as those we had already discovered. At the end of an exhausting day at the computer, I finally asked myself, "What in the world is this compulsive behavior all about? What in the world are you doing?"

Immediately, I knew the answer. I was looking for the perfect doctor, the perfect clinic, the perfect plan that I could entrust with my son's life. I was looking for someone more trustworthy than God.

Ahh, there it was. I was looking for someone more trustworthy than the God who had allowed this tumor into our lives. This wasn't about research. It was about a struggle to trust. A struggle that had left me looking for something I would never find on the computer screen in "search."

▶ Has your pain shaken or, better said, reshaped your relationship with God? In these troubling times, where are you looking for help or security apart from your faith?

I believe. Help my unbelief. God, I am scared and angry. Mostly scared.

✣✤ The same old struggle

For some reason I thought I would be immune to my ordinary life struggles as I was going through this trauma. But there it was again: the stepchild syndrome.

I have an old high school friend who struggles financially. A single mom, she has nobly chosen a job that maximizes her time with her children but brings in an income that allows her to barely scrape by. It is a trade-off she has consciously chosen and bravely accepts.

The other day she called me on the phone to celebrate God's amazing grace. Needing a new roof on her home for months, she had just recently gotten a bid that indicated she would need several thousand dollars to fix it. Money she simply did not have. To her amazement, she received a call from her pastor that someone in her church had anonymously given the money to fix her roof. She was tearfully and humbly grateful. I was, too.

Later that evening, after I snapped at my husband for something really silly, I began to backtrack in my day to find out what had shifted inside me to create such irritation. Only then did I realize that my old "friend" that I call "the stepchild syndrome" had returned.

Though I was confident that I would never wish for my friend to have *not* received the generous gift she had been given, the fact that God had spared her such a burden somehow seemed to make my burden feel that much weightier. Why didn't God bless us in such a way? Our mounting medical bills were at least as much as her roof! Why is it that we don't receive that kind of help? I felt like a stepchild of God.

Though I cannot identify for you the source of this struggle, I know it as a longstanding battle I fight from time to time, usually with success. And I will fight it again this time.

But why did it surface now? For some reason I thought I would be immune to the same old struggle.

▶ Can you identify any familiar and not so lovely "ordinary" struggles that have been a part of this "extraordinary" season?

Here I am again, God. It is a good thing your mercies are new every morning. I seem to need a lot these days. Here I am again.

Vow making

One of my favorite factoids about Scripture is that there are more psalms of lament than any other kind of psalm. That fact communicates many things to me. For instance, it says to me that God knows life is hard. These songs were the worship hymnal for the Jewish community. Much of what the people experienced in life was suffering; so much of what they expressed to God was lament. It also says to me that God values honest, authentic relationship more than some dressed up version of my life that I might imagine to be God's preference. Lament can and indeed must be a part of real relationship with God. I get that.

But there is another aspect to many of these psalms that I have had little experience with: vow making. Many times when the psalmist was in a particularly tight spot, he would make a special promise to God that later, after God had rescued him once again, he would then fulfill. Reading again in the psalms recently about vow making, it sounded a bit like the bargaining stage of grief to me. Well, I figured, whatever the motivation, it was worth a shot.

The example of vow making that came to mind for me was Hannah's promise to God that if God would give her a son, she would give him right back to God. Now my desperate plea had everything to do with my son also, but since he is an adult, I cannot imagine that giving him back to God would be a very meaningful sacrifice.

What did I have to give to God? Was there something connected to my plea for rescue that I could offer as a vow? The only thing that came to mind was this story that I am recording for you now. Even before it is finished, before I know how it will end, or what twists and turns it may take before we will reach the end, I am making the choice to give the story of this uninvited journey back to God. As honestly as I can, I desire to write this part of my life: the good, the bad, and even the ugly. My faith tells me than any story, when given to God, can become a thing of beauty.

I sense in my soul that this vow making is serious business; that I probably have very little idea of what I am getting myself into. Yet, I am a mother desperate to see God's saving and healing graces in this moment of pain, grief, and illness for her son. So, I am a woman willing to risk vow making.

▶ How do you feel about vow making? Have you sought to bargain with God in other ways?

It worked for Hannah, God. I give you what I have. It is all I have. Do what you will with it; only heal my son, God. Please, God, heal my son.

❧ Feeling our way

As we wait for films to be shipped and specialists to return from vacation, the day-to-day rhythm changes. We are at least two weeks from a final decision on surgery, and a friend and old Little League baseball coach of Bob's has offered him a job doing some filing at his law office.

Today was his first day on the job and he arrived back at home after working for five hours. When I inquired about why he was home so soon, he said he got tired of working so he left. From his conversations with his employer, they were not assuming he would necessarily be working full time, just whatever he wanted. I was assuming full time. Why not?

Where is the line? Will someone please clarify the rules for me? How much time do you get off from life for having a brain tumor even if you have no symptoms that impact your ability to work? Is this a moment of a parentally imposed work week or do I let it slide?

Am I enabling or offering needed compassion? How much of the laissez-faire attitude is tumor location or how much is escape or the need for space in which to cope or just a simple preference for pleasure? I don't want him to be overwhelmed. Neither do I want him to feel guilty. But is a little gratitude expressed in cash support too much to ask? I mean, that's a real question: Is it too much to ask? Maybe it is.

How much of this bone-breaking financial burden does he need to bear for the sake of his adulthood? I wrote a check for $3,275.50 this morning to repay his living allowance loan from this un-semester. That was our money, painstakingly saved, to go to England for our twenty-fifth anniversary. We have never been to England.

I handled the moment with little grace or wisdom, a lot of fear and even more frustration.

Will someone please clarify the rules for me? How much time do you get off from life for having a brain tumor?

I'm feeling my way along this unknowable path. I know he is, too. Together. We are feeling our way.

▶ Have there been difficult relational moments in your journey that you have not handled well?

Help me, God. This is not who I want to be.

Stark terror

Sometimes, as an ex-nurse, I just know too much for my own good…or at least my own comfort.

As the tumor journey moved forward and Bob pondered the costliness of potential blindness, he was leaning toward the conservative approach of simply watching the mass. We knew from his symptoms that the tumor was either not growing at all or very slightly. Before finalizing his decision, however, he felt he needed to know the composition of the tumor more definitively. So, he decided to pursue a less invasive endoscopic biopsy.

We made an appointment with the second neurosurgeon, explored his minimally invasive approach, addressed potential risks, and were feeling very confident that this was a relatively low-risk procedure.

The surgery was to take two to three hours and we were thankful for friends and family to keep us occupied as we waited. Two hours into the surgery we were encouraged by an update that all was well and they would soon be done. We were instructed not to leave the waiting room because the doctor would be out shortly.

As time ticked on and the doctor did not come, I tried to divorce myself from my nursing/chaplain sense that all was probably not well anymore. Ninety minutes later, Dr. Parsons walked out, devoid of his usual broad smile and jovial demeanor. We followed him to a consultation room.

"Technically, the surgery went very well." Immediately, I knew I did not like that word "technically." It seems that our son was having a very difficult time waking up and they did not know why. In the last half-hour, though he had finally begun to respond to some commands, he was completely mute. Again, the doctor had no explanation, only vague conjecture. Based on those guesses, they began some medicines. He was sending Bob to the Intensive Care Unit with the expectation that whatever had gone wrong would fix itself. We were welcome to go see him.

When we got to ICU, it was even worse than I had anticipated. His small measure of responsiveness had evaporated and my twenty-three-year-old son lay completely unresponsive in the bed, even unresponsive to pain. He was barely breathing. The nurse and assisting doctor were preparing for more testing. As an ex-nurse, I knew too much for my own good, or at least my own comfort. All I could feel was stark terror.

▶ Have you experienced any moments of stark terror on your journey? What moments have been the most unsettling or even soul-shattering?

O, God. O, God. O, God.

✢ Too "mind full" to be mindful

At one point earlier in that frightening biopsy day, I set out to walk to our hotel room to give our younger daughter directions to the waiting room. As you might imagine, the 5:45 AM pre-surgery arrival time was a bit extreme for her teenage body. Unfamiliar with the hospital, I asked directions of the volunteer before I headed out.

At this moment in our day, I thought I was coping pretty well. I felt calm inside, not particularly anxious. After all, it was supposed to be a routine procedure even if it was brain surgery. I conversed freely with our pastor and my brother and sister-in-law who had come to wait with us. I was even able to plan with some forethought about the day.

Following the directions I had been given, I found myself walking along a narrow driveway, walled on both sides by construction projects. I thought to myself, "This isn't very safe. They should have signs warning people to not come this way."

Sure enough, as I exited onto a larger drive, a policeman stopped me and told me I shouldn't be walking there. He said there were signs.

Sadly, rather than acknowledging my error, I am ashamed to say that I "blamed" the volunteer who had given me directions and silently (thankfully not openly) doubted there were really any signs posted. You see, I am a very good sign reader. And I had seen none.

On my way back and taking a safer route, I did indeed confirm the presence of not one but two very large "NO PEDESTRIAN" signs that I must have walked right past. What was up with that?

Whether I had realized it or not, my mind and heart were so full I was no longer able to be mindful of my surroundings. That was a frightening thought for me. What else had I missed? Also, it was so unlike me to play the blame game. What was really happening inside my soul?

I began to doubt my sense of calm. Was it true peace or simply the deadness of vulnerable emotion being banished from this moment by fear? In any event, I knew from years of compassionately working with stressed families that however I was coping for now, I was doing the best I could. I would simply have to accept the fact that, at least for now, I was too "mind full" to be mindful.

▶ How has your awareness level changed during this time of crisis or loss? Are you more vigilant? Less aware? Both?

Clearly, God, I need help. Though sadly, I am likely only vaguely aware of just how much I need!

❧ My confession about prayer

The older I get, the less I know about prayer. For years I thought I knew how to pray, when to pray, what was my part, what was God's part, and how to get results from prayer. I don't know how it happened, but I don't know any of that anymore.

How does prayer work? Why does it work? When does it work?

One might conclude that knowing less about the process might mean I pray less. Not so.

When our son was first diagnosed with this brain tumor, one of my first responses was to ask for massive amounts of prayer. Again, not because I know why or how it will make a difference, but because I believe that somehow it will make a difference.

In ICU that day, I was torn between being with our son and going downstairs to e-mail the many praying friends who were waiting for news. When he left the room for a CAT scan, I found a computer. After a brief description of our current circumstance, again, I asked for prayer… immediate prayer.

When Bob returned from the CAT scan less than thirty minutes later, he began to respond. Ever so slowly, over the next many hours, he began to awaken.

Walking back to our hotel room later that night, my daughter and I spoke about prayer. Even as the grateful recipient of such prayer that day, I felt odd confessing to her that I still could not say I knew any more about prayer…how it works, why it works, when it works. Somehow, strangely, those things just did not seem to matter.

What I do know is this: I know that somehow prayer works, somehow things change, somehow goodness comes. I know I'm drawn to prayer. I know I need to pray.

Limited as it might be, this is my confession about prayer.

▶ What do you believe about prayer? Has your perspective been changed by this journey of pain?

You have heard my cry, O God. Thank you. Thank you.

Fearfully and wonderfully made

When I was pregnant with each of our three children, I often thought of the words of Psalm 139: "You are fearfully and wonderfully made." I continue to be amazed at the mysterious wonder of human creation!

But I have concluded recently that there is a downside to that truth. We are so complexly designed that there are still many, many, many areas that medicine must leave more to mystery than to the mathematical ways of knowing in science. Such is the case with our son's tumor. Seated within the deepest parts of the brain, literally in the very center of his head, his tumor is probably rooted very close to his hypothalamus.

Now, there are a few reasons why you have probably never heard of such a place in your brain. For one, amazingly, few things go wrong in these ultra-sensitive structures. God saw fit to keep them tucked in tight, cushioned from harm. Secondly, they are also so deeply isolated that they are hard to study. And thirdly, and probably most significantly, they are pretty mysterious.

The hypothalamus is not a structure unto itself as much as a grouping of cells that line a portion of the third ventricle of the brain. These cells are located in a certain place in most folks but not necessarily in that precise place in others. For instance, our son's MRI shows the place where the hypothalamus is usually located as tumor, but he has no obvious symptoms of hypothalamus damage, so maybe his is somewhere else. Maybe.

The hypothalamus controls such vague yet core functions as sleep/wakefulness, thirst, personality drive, and one's experience of hot/cold. If one's hypothalamus is "hot" or irritated, one can have fits of rage. If it is "cold" or has diminished blood supply, one can become biologically euphoric or indolent. Maybe.

When our son did not wake up for hours after surgery, the doctors thought maybe it was due to hypothalamic irritation. Maybe.

Wouldn't it be nice if medicine, especially life-and-death medicine, were always like simple arithmetic? Maybe.

Perhaps, ultimately, mystery is even more trustworthy than math. After all, we are fearfully and wonderfully made.

▸ What aspects of your current journey seem too uncertain, fuzzy, or mysterious to you? How are you dealing with them?

God, I glimpse trust and comfort in this mystery, but right now, it just makes me more afraid.

Just let it cut

I guess we all have our ways of remembering things. Oddly, even though I am a writer, I tend to remember words and concepts in terms of images. I can rarely accurately quote someone, but I retain an idea I have read about through images that stick in my mind.

A number of years ago, I heard a woman speak who said something like (notice the inexact quote!) "the channel that pain cuts in your heart, joy can later fill." At the time I heard that idea I was intrigued by it but had little experience with such things. Nevertheless, the image stuck.

My inexperience was not because I had not encountered painful situations; it was just that I had consistently refused to allow that pain access to tender parts of my heart. I chose instead to hold it in my mind and body, an approach that seemed to work for many years. I should have guessed what God was up to when I encountered such an intriguing idea. How tricky of God to use my mind to finally access my heart.

Over the last ten plus years, since encountering that truth, I have begun to live with more pain and more joy. Welcoming pain has increased my joy; to the degree to which I have held grief at bay, I have also refused joy. Though I do not understand it, they are indeed connected.

Yet, even knowing all that, each time I encounter pain, I must actively choose to engage it. It has been more than a week since our son's biopsy and the terrifying day we spent waiting for him to wake up. This morning as I sat in the chapel, I let the pain of this tumor journey cut a new and deeper channel in my tender and hurting heart. I sat for a long time with that bloody image in my mind, tears on my cheeks, and profound pain in my heart. Pain whose cutting work I welcomed as an odd friend.

I do not know when or where or how the new capacity for joy will appear. I do not know what kind of joy will fill that larger space. But I know it will come, somewhere, somehow, sometime. Because today I made the choice to welcome my pain and say to my heart, "Just let it cut."

▶ How would you describe your current relationship with your pain? Do you feel it fully in the moment? Stiff-arm it? Take it in over time? Let it cut? Deny it exists? Intellectualize it?

"...weeping may linger for the night, but joy comes with the morning." Psalm 30:5

❧ Emotionally fragile

I find that language is often very revealing. Sometimes, it says more than we know. Sometimes it does more than we know, too, shaping our perspectives and choices.

The last few days I have described my current life experience to friends as "emotionally fragile." It's an expression I picked up from a friend and basically means I just might burst into tears at any moment. Reflecting on that phrase today, I thought to myself, "What a misnomer!"

Let me explain. Working as a hospital chaplain, I am sometimes amused by which patients the nurses refer to us and which they do not. We often receive calls about emotionally healthy, appropriately coping people who are found to be crying uncontrollably when given devastating news from a doctor. On the other hand, in routine floor visits, we sometimes encounter less healthy individuals in similar circumstances who are in the throes of deep denial. Though these individuals need our help much more, we rarely receive a referral on their behalf. They just look so strong.

Even as I have been labeling myself "emotionally fragile," I have probably been responding with more health, strength, and maturity than ever before in my life. My tendency to "break down" (again, note the deceptive language) is evidence of significant healing in my life. There were many, many years in which I could not cry at all, much less cry in the presence of someone else!

Admittedly, there is also a sense of fragility and vulnerability that comes with this expression of emotion. I have just given those around me critical data about what matters in my life and how they can hurt me if they so desire.

But what is missed by the expression "emotionally fragile" is the greater goodness of the choice to grieve. Because I am grieving, I can heal. When I grieve in the presence of others, I can receive comfort. Those choices both reveal inner emotional strength and grow the same. They are anything but fragile.

So, maybe I need to come up with some new language…not to seek to deny the vulnerable elements of my current state but to remind myself that even when I am at a point in life when I just might burst into tears at any moment, I am anything but emotionally fragile.

▶ Have you had experiences of being "emotionally fragile"? Have others around you? How do you see those moments?

Thank you for tears, God. Keep me safe as I cry them, and please, please use them to make me strong. I need to be strong.

❧ It's just what I do

My husband, Robert, washes dishes. My son, Bob, watches funny movies. And I write. It's just what I do when I'm trying to reorder my world…to make sense of chaos, to cope with pain. It's just what I do.

Oddly, it took me a good forty-five years to notice that I am a writer. In my family of origin, the act and art of writing were rarely discussed. We weren't a very talkative bunch, so wordsmithing didn't hold much value in our family economy. In fact, few of the fine arts were on the radar screen of my parents' experience, and consequently they weren't on mine.

So, how, might you ask, did you conclude that you are a writer? Like many other profound revelations in my life, it was one of those core truths that others saw in me long before I recognized it in myself. For instance, in high school I did competitive ready-writing, not because I recognized myself as a writer but because my teacher asked me to. A data point long forgotten. For years, the only things I wrote were research papers for nursing school, vacation Bible school curricula and notes to teachers for my children.

When I returned to graduate school at age forty, my professors complimented my writing repeatedly…words I easily dismissed as flattery designed to keep me paying the tuition. I learned the value of journaling as a self-reflection technique and used it often. I found that I enjoyed putting my ideas into words, but still was far from owning my ability as a writer.

At some point, though, I decided maybe all those compliments had been more than simple flattery. Working on a variety of committees in the last several years, I noticed that others began to rely on my writing abilities to shape direction for the groups. Gathering thoughts into words came easily for me…almost so easily that I dismissed it as a real contribution. (Often the case when we are operating in our area of giftedness).

At the same time, I began to realize that I am a writer not because of what I put on paper, but more so because it is just what I do. When I encounter life in all its various forms of joys and sorrows, I begin to shape my experience into ideas and concepts. Then I connect those with other truths I know and other experiences I have had and *boom*, there it is…an article pops out almost fully formed. I never realized I thought that way, much less that it might be a part of my unique giftedness.

You see, quite simply, it's just what I do.

▶ What do you do to order your world? How is it working for you?

I am grateful, God, that even in all this mess, something familiar is still working for me.

❧ Shut up and keep pushing

Growing up with a mother whose passion was labor and delivery nursing, I heard many birth stories: good births, difficult births, unique births, funny births, tragic births. Perhaps I inherited a bit of her passion for it all, because my own birthing experiences have been core stories for me, treasured moments that have continued to inform my life.

Each labor was unique. The first was induced, fairly short for a first baby, but concluded with a forceps delivery after a fruitless two plus hours of pushing. The second was relatively easy, with the notable exception of a series of sequential contractions that almost killed me (not literally) and sent my doctor racing across town just in time to catch our first daughter. I learned the fine art of panting to avoid pushing as we awaited his arrival.

My third labor was slow and steady. I walked lap after lap in the hospital corridor, even through transition. When I quit walking, our second girl quit coming. The delivery process was just as painstakingly slow. At one point, I lost it, screaming, "Just tell me how much longer this is going to last. If you can just tell me, I'll do it." (As if I had the choice to quit!)

My wise, steady, and utterly kind doctor knew just what I needed. She got right in my face and said with great firmness and clarity, "You know we can't tell you that. Just shut up and keep pushing." So I did.

There have been many moments in my life since then when I have heard once again the echo of her wise and necessary voice. "Just shut up and keep pushing." Painful moments as a young mom when I was over-whelmed by the needs of three preschool children. Frustrated moments when I was trying to complete a paper for graduate school while negoti-ating the needs of three teenagers and a husband. Exhausted moments as a hospital chaplain when there was a code called at the end of a long day. "Just shut up and keep pushing."

Yesterday, we had our follow-up appointment with the neurosurgeon. I was thankful to hear that our son is healing well. I was thankful for a definitive diagnosis of a juvenile pilocytic astrocytoma, a very slow-growing tumor. I was thankful for the possibility that the tumor might respond to chemo or radiation. I was just somehow not prepared for the recommendation that we see three more specialists.

In the midst of weary tears, I heard once again just what I needed to hear: "Just shut up and keep pushing."

▶ What moments in this journey have called for the most resilience or endur-ance? What has kept you going?

This is so hard, God. And I am so tired.

❧ New gray hair

I got my hair cut today for the first time since this tumor journey began. My usual stylist had moved out of town and I just did not have the energy to find a new one. Post-biopsy, things have finally settled down enough for me to focus on such niceties of life. At least I'm trying to refocus.

I'm pretty sure the number of gray hairs in my head has at least doubled in the last few months. As a former nurse, I never put much credence in the thought that stress causes gray hair, but now I'm beginning to wonder.

My new stylist educated me a bit on this change taking place in my scalp. It seems gray hairs are much coarser and unruly because they have no pigment. They are, if you will, hair in the rawest form, stripped of all that generally makes hair manageable.

Now, that observation fits my soul at this moment. It reminds me of those moments in ICU barely a week ago: stark terror. Raw, coarse, unruly, stripped of all that makes life appear manageable. It seems fitting to be carrying small evidences of those moments with me now. I don't know if I will ever look at my son and not remember the possibilities that played out in my mind that afternoon when he could not wake up. Yes, thankfully, we are beyond that moment now. But no, I will not forget.

This week as I have been back in my regular routine encountering people who love me, few have been willing to see my gray hair. They only want to celebrate how well our son is doing…indeed, something worthy of *great* thanksgiving and celebration. But can't they see my new gray hair?

I've decided that I like the gray. It reminds me of the woman I am becoming, the wise and gentle person I am seeking within myself. Authentic to the point of seeming raw. Free to hear and obey my strange and holy God to the point of seeming unruly. Strong and enduring enough to be labeled as coarse.

Yes, I've decided I like my new gray hair.

▶ Have you experienced places in this journey where you have felt raw or coarse or unruly?

God, I do like the woman I am becoming, but please, can't we find another way to incite such growth?

❧ Lizard-eye emotion

Have you ever experienced two completely opposite sets of feelings simultaneously? Perhaps the emotional version of the way a lizard can look in two different directions simultaneously?

About the same time our tumor journey began, a good friend of mine moved away to seminary. Carlene and I had known each other only a few years but had formed a strong friendship due to many common experiences in our past.

Carlene's route to becoming a pastor had been a long and hard-fought journey. She had grown up in traditions that were uncomfortable with women assuming those roles, yet her sense of calling persisted. Though for years she had worked for change within those systems, in the end God led her to the Episcopal Church, which welcomed her without reservation. Needless to say, she was ecstatic about her move: a dream come true. Sadly, at the same time it became apparent that, for unrelated reasons, her marriage of thirty plus years was dissolving: a nightmare realized. Lizard-eye emotion.

For years I had longed to publish a book. Interestingly, I remember that desire being present long before I would ever dare to call myself a writer. While many of Carlene's battles had been external, most of mine had come from within. Finally conquering my fears, and aided by the miracle of a daring and visionary publisher, I signed my first book contract the very day our son was diagnosed with his brain tumor. Lizard-eye emotion.

What can I say about lizard-eye emotions? For sure, they can make you feel dizzy and at times even crazy. However they arrive, the real question is: How can you deal with lizard-eye emotion? Rationally, I somehow tend to think they will neutralize one another. But, experientially, what has happened is not so much a neutral meeting in the center to mix or blend, but a sense of being stretched by the extremes. It feels as if my capacity for experiencing all kinds of emotion is being expanded. I am forced by those extremes to live more completely in the moment of whatever that minute brings. Like it or not, the next minute is likely to be wildly different when you are living in the midst of lizard-eye emotion.

▶ Have you ever experienced "lizard-eye" emotions along the way? Have they felt fragmenting? Soul expanding? Both?

Grow me, God, and gather me into more and more of the person I am.

🌿 Washed with the water of the Word

Among various scholars and different denominations, there is much debate about just exactly what it is that makes Scripture so special. Some point to its endurance. Why has this book remained so intact and relatively unaltered for so long, with generation after generation choosing to preserve these certain words?

Some point to Scripture's broad appeal. People from many different centuries and many cultures have attested to its sacred value in their lives. How is it that these words written by people so far away and long ago still speak to me? Others have extensive apologetically-focused arguments that highlight the details and care of its creation. Some see its formation as a mystical, spiritually dictated process.

Interestingly, no matter how you get to the conclusion, most people will agree that Scripture is somehow special. One of the most intriguing aspects of its specialness to me is expressed in the phrase: washed with the water of the Word. Perhaps it is because I tend to be so visually connected to words.

This morning as I recited the psalms with my Benedictine monk friends, that phrase came to mind.

I arrived weary from a hard day yesterday. I had had my fill of the tumor journey and spent the prior evening in grief. Rather than feeling as if I had been purged and healed by my grief, I woke this morning still tired of it, grieving anew over how disoriented my life has become because of this unexpected and unwelcome twist in the road.

I often come to Saturday Morning Prayer and so I know these particular psalms by heart. As we moved from one to the other, the words felt as if they were washing over my inflamed, hurting, and angry soul as a healing balm. As I closed my eyes, I didn't follow the individual meaning of sentences as much as catch the rhythm of the words and phrases…repeatedly I heard "cry" and "cry out," "wait," "the Lord," "salvation," "praise," "heard," "strength," "song," "my king," "victory."

Ever so slowly, my world was once again righted…not fixed, informed, resolved or released from pain and confusion, but re-oriented, perhaps even refreshed, in such a profound way that I was freed to move forward, washed with the water of the Word.

▸ What forces or sources tend to re-orient you when you are confused, overwhelmed, or writhing? Scripture? Prayer? Other Books? Experiences? Places? People? Music?

God, I am amazed by the many and varied ways you touch me with your comfort. Thank you.

Like a weaned child

As a mother, I enjoyed the privilege of nursing all three of our children. I savored the bonding that took place in those quiet and intimate moments together.

That personal experience has made Psalm 131 especially healing for me.

But I have calmed and quieted my soul,
like a weaned child with its mother;
my soul is like the weaned child that is with me.

I remember the raw neediness of my babies in the early days, the inability to wait and trust, the demand of their cries and the desperation of their spirits. I recall their grabbiness and harassed anxiety as they began to nurse. Their very lives depended on me. As far as they knew, I was their only potential source of food.

I remember the trust that developed between my children and me. Over time, they learned that, indeed, I would be available to them, not necessarily on demand, but when needed. They learned to wait. They developed a willingness to abide with their hunger (to a limited extent, of course!). By the time they were weaned, they could sit quietly in my lap even when it was mealtime. Their trust became a stronger force than their hunger.

That is the message I hear echoed in these precious verses. They call me to a kind of rest and peace that is not grounded in the absence of hunger but in the presence of a trusting relationship. When hard times come my way, I almost always begin in that place of grabby harassed anxiety. I pray ceaselessly, begging, and at times demanding a response from God. Such has been the case with this tumor journey.

Yet, now, I find myself drawn to God's lap. I remember all the years that God has faithfully nursed me. My frantic wordy prayers cease. I am full of trust and the unrushed willingness to wait.

My prayer becomes simply sitting quietly, like a weaned child.

▶ In this moment, are you feeling more like a trusting weaned child or an anxious, hungry, screaming infant?

"Return, O my soul, to your rest, for the Lord has dealt bountifully with you."
Psalm 116:7

Mountains and molehills

Some folks might have thought he was making a mountain out of a molehill. When Bob mentioned to the doctor at a routine check-up that he had little facial hair at age twenty-three, most men would say, "Just thank your lucky stars."

Yet, this molehill really *was* a mountain. That small gender-specific data point revealed a brain tumor that has turned out to be no small issue. It has also changed my perspective on molehills.

Now, to some extent, that may not be a good thing. I have found myself in recent months concerned about just about every little ache or pain in my own body or anyone else's. I took our younger daughter, Betsy, to our son's neuro-ophthalmologist the other day because one of her pupils was bigger than the other. Though our local doctor had assured me that the problem was simply a painless migraine, I had to be sure it wasn't another mountain disguised as a molehill. I am hoping that time will restore my perspective on such moments.

But this tumor journey has also brought some positive experiences of molehills becoming mountains. For instance, who would have thought it would mean so much to receive silent, knowing hugs from Madison, week after week? Who would have assumed that a pug puppy could bring consolation? Who would imagine such concrete comfort from altar flowers, freshly arranged and hand delivered?

Who would have believed that such molehills of kindness can make even mountains like tumors seem so much smaller? Mountains and molehills.

▶ Have any molehills in your life become mountains recently? Which have brought unexpected pain? Which have brought comfort?

I long for some sense of balance, God. My world seems so very off-kilter.

Off the prayer list

When do you take your name off the prayer list? When can the crisis no longer be called a crisis? When does it become a new normal?

These are some of the questions arising in me this weekend. As we continue to ponder our options, it is looking more and more as if our son will choose to do nothing in terms of treatment for his tumor. At this point in time, the risks of treatment outweigh the benefits. Thankfully, the few symptoms he has can be easily remedied with medicines.

But surely, the fact that he still has a tumor lodged in the middle of his brain is worthy of some sense of crisis…and therefore prayer, isn't it? If this thing grows at all we may be in *big* trouble in a hurry. It feels like realizing that your house is built on the edge of a sinkhole and you never know when that cavernous hole might decide to grow! How can we possibly move away from our sense of crisis, from our fervent prayer?

On the other hand, how can we *not*? One known fact about human life is that we have an internal driver that continually seeks to establish a sense of homeostasis, an internal level of sorts, both physically and emotionally. Whether my motherly instincts like it or not, we are all moving toward this "new normal" even as I silently rail against it.

So, why am I so reluctant to let go of crisis mode? Perhaps I think it keeps me safer, more alert and able to defend those I love, and myself, from danger. What an illusion! Of the potential dangers around us, my degree of alertness affects so few, so very few. Perhaps I am afraid of returning to my life as I "left" it just a few months back. With my last child preparing to leave for college and my first book being published, there is much grief, challenge, excitement, and fear just ahead of me on my path. Perhaps I had simply wanted this tumor journey to end differently, tied neatly with a bow on top, with the tumor cured and no threats or ill effects remaining. Maybe I'm trying to hold out for the ending I prefer.

In any case, it is becoming clear that, for now, it is time to be taken off the prayer list.

► Do you find yourself fighting against establishing a "new normal"? Or do you welcome it? Or both?

Though I want tidy packages and long-term guarantees, God, you don't seem so inclined. Help me see the goodness you see. Help me trust even when I can't.

❧ My need to know

One of the precious gifts in my present life is having a few good friends who challenge me. One such friend, John, recently invited me to simply give up my "need to know."

Though I was intrigued by his invitation, I intuitively sensed that accepting this invitation would be far more difficult than it might appear at first glance. Give up the need to know all there is to know about my son's tumor? Give up the need to know all potential risks or benefits of any given treatment path? How could I? Sadly, that was just the beginning of a very long list of things I felt I needed to know.

Give up my need to know whether this tumor will grow or not?

Give up my need to know whether or not my son will go blind?

Give up my need to know where the money will come from to pay these mounting medical bills?

Give up my need to know if my son will eventually need surgery?

Give up my need to know if he will be able to restart and finish law school?

Give up my need to know if he will father children?

Give up my need to know how his bills will be paid when we can no longer cover him on our insurance?

Give up my need to know how he will cope emotionally with this burden?

Give up my need to know if he will be able to find a mate who will be willing to bear this with him?

Give up my need to know if I will be strong enough to bear this ordeal?

Give up my need to know how much of his behavior is tumor and how much is just him?

Give up my need to know when this will be over?

Somewhere along the line I realized my own foolishness. As if I could possibly ever have truly definitive answers to any of the above questions. So, why then, am I so enticed by this need to know?

In part, I think this drive to know is a noble thing…part of the image of God playing out in my soul. In part, it is my desire to secure a life for myself apart from God, a decidedly ignoble and utterly frustrating endeavor.

I'm working on embracing my present and forever dependence, letting go of my need to know.

▶ Make your own list of things you feel you need to know.

Perhaps, God, all I really need to know is you?

❧ Collateral impact

Main Entry: **collateral damage**
Function: *noun*
: injury inflicted on something other than an intended target; *specifically*
: civilian casualties of a military operation
(Merriam-Webster Online Dictionary, 2003)

On this tumor journey there is the grief directly related to the tumor and, aside from that, there is collateral grief. Those are the losses associated with dealing with the tumor…the ripple effect if you will. As a chaplain, one of the things I have learned is that to grieve well over an event means to also grieve over all the collateral losses. I just never knew it could be so massive and so very painful. The first step is to begin to name it…ugh. Does naming it make it more real or does it just feel that way?

Among the things sacrificed to these ripples…

A quiet house in which to write

A tidy house, free from clutter

Many dollars and all the things those dollars could have purchased

Restful nights

Harmonious relationships

A trip to England

Weeks of time

A first year of law school as planned

Feelings of wholeness

Peace of mind

Strangely, Proverbs 14:4 comes to mind.
Where no oxen are, the manger is clean,
But much increase comes from the strength of an ox.

I cannot escape this wisdom—collateral grief is real but so is collateral blessing—things like…

Unexpected time with Bob, the simple joy of his presence

Uninvited growth of character and faith that accompanies such journeys

Newborn strength from the unique resistance strength-training program called "bearing new life burdens"

Indeed, there are two different kinds of collateral impact.

▶ What are your collateral losses? Your collateral blessings?

God, give me eyes to see and a heart willing to feel the full breadth of this journey.

✤ Bits of incarnation

I've been thinking a lot lately about the idea of incarnation…not just the reality of Jesus coming to earth as a God-Man, but also the fact that He is here today, incarnate in the body of the church—me and you. What does that look like in real time? Day to day? How does it play out in a life? Specifically, in my life?

One of the reasons it has been difficult for me to own writing as a spiritual calling, a part of Jesus incarnate in my world, is because I enjoy it so much. There is perhaps some vestige of legalism within me that says it would just be too good to be true for this to actually be kingdom *work*.

As I have said before, the beginning of the tumor journey happened to coincide with my first book contract. Thankfully, I had completed the manuscript at that point. As friends heard about these life events, more than one commented, "Well, I guess we all know the subject matter of your second book." I wondered at their remarks but did not really take them seriously because I had something altogether different in mind for my next endeavor.

Yet, several weeks into this journey, I began to recognize my need to "write my way through" these strange and painful experiences. Finally, prompted by a desire to make a vow to God in connection with my plea for our son's healing, I began to write. Immediately, I came up with twenty titles for vignettes at a single sitting! Was this pump primed or what?

As I sat to write, the words just poured out, flowed amazingly. It felt so natural, organic, if you will, as if I were listening and responding to a deep, deep rhythm as I worked. Again, I wondered, could this actually be a calling? Could this really be what faithfulness looks like for me? These words felt so healing for me personally…might they also be something that could be healing to others?

Again prompted by my vow to offer this story as kingdom work, I sent the first few pages to a friend who is in the midst of a particularly painful time. She called me the other day to let me know how very much these words had helped her. "I cried my way through. It was so healing." Perhaps it is true…perhaps these simple words really are healing bits of incarnation.

▶ What moments of goodness have you found in this week of your journey? Have any come from within yourself? Have any blessed those around you?

Lord, speak to me, so I can speak in living echoes of your love.

❧ I know I'm stressed

I know I'm stressed when…

> I am frustrated by the mounting number of different shampoos and soaps in the shower stall.

> I realize after the fact that I've eaten four pieces of candy before 11 AM.

> My children ask, "What's for dinner?" and I reply, "Whatever you can find"…for the fourth evening in a row.

> I check my e-mail several times a day hoping for some outside force to surge through the lines to rescue me.

> I find myself complaining to everyone I meet about my lack of money.

I fold the pile of clothes on my bed one or two pieces at a time, too distracted to complete even that small task.

My stomach muscles resist when I try to take a deep breath.

I cannot find time to write a thank-you note.

The sound of my children's laughter irritates me.

My bed does not get made for a full week.

The house becomes messier and messier and messier with each passing day.

I dry the same load of clothes four times.

I have not picked up a book in weeks.

I watch solved-in-an-hour crime shows all evening on TV.

Oddly, the thought of desperately needed self-care is the last thing I tend to consider even when I know I'm stressed.

▶ Are you stressed? How do you know?

My soul is shaking in fear, God, vibrating from the inside out. I need your help. I need your touch.

Oh by the way…

Oh by the way…four little words followed by earthquakes of varying proportions creating tsunamis of the soul.

The first doctor said…Oh by the way…you may want to drop out of law school.

The second doctor said…Oh by the way…this is not an ordinary pituitary tumor.

The third doctor said…Oh by the way…to simply do a biopsy will mean a mini-craniotomy.

The fourth doctor said…Oh by the way…if you operate on this thing, it might mess with your personality.

The fifth doctor said…Oh by the way…there's a five to ten percent chance of blindness with the surgery.

The sixth doctor said…Oh by the way…this supplement will make him sterile so you might want to think about sperm banking.

The sperm bank said…Oh by the way…in addition to the $400 charge today, you need to get this additional lab work that insurance won't cover either. It's another $276.

The surgeon said…Oh by the way…the procedure went well but he's not really waking up and we aren't sure why.

The insurance company said…Oh by the way…his second day in the hospital has been "non-certified."

The seventh doctor said…Oh by the way…there's a two to three percent chance that the radiation could cause new and more aggressive brain tumors to grow.

No wonder I feel as if I am drowning.

Will you rescue me, God? All the breakers and waves are rushing over me. Please, Lord, rescue me…oh by the way.

▶ Name any moments from your recent journey which have contained a sense of "Oh by the way."

Oh, by the way, God, can you hear me? Are you listening?

Lost perspective

Yesterday was definitely a day of lost perspective. It seemed to me to be such an odd moment for such abject discouragement. We had spent a large part of the morning in Houston again, meeting with a lovely and competent radiation oncologist. She had informed, engaged, and helped us a great deal. Basically the news was good. If the tumor grows, we will definitely consider radiation as one of the preferred treatment options. As our tradition dictates, we had lunch and drove home.

So why then have I lost perspective now? Yesterday we got a *huge* credit card bill. As I went through it one item at a time, I could not disagree with any of the decisions behind the spending…yet, at the same time, it feels as if the money thing is *totally* out of control. Hundreds and thousands of dollars floating away…the well is very, very, very close to dry. When will the bleeding stop? It's just out of control.

Ahh, maybe that's it. Life out of control. It feels as if my life is out of control. My home, money, dreams, and time have all been given over to this monstrous tumor journey.

How hard I fought all last evening to re-establish some semblance of control. Barking at my children and husband, and most of all at myself… all to no avail. If regaining control is the only answer to this problem, I am sunk for sure.

Lost perspective…I guess there are really two ways to see that expression. One, that I have lost my perspective on the world; the other, that I have a "lost" perspective, that I feel as if I am lost. That thought strikes a deep chord in me. I do feel as if I am lost, alone, abandoned, afraid, unsure, surrounded by unfamiliar territory without anyone to help me.

Why do I feel so alone? I have friends and family who would love to help. Why do I choose to bear so much alone?

Though I have no answer, at least this feels like a healing path…far more helpful than my fruitless battle for control.

I am reminded that when you are lost in the woods, wisdom sometimes says to stop, stay where you are and wait to be rescued. Friends are looking for you, eager to save you from your lost perspective.

▶ When have you lost perspective along the way? Or do you simply feel lost?

"Wait for the Lord; be strong, and let your heart take courage; wait for the Lord!"
Psalm 27:14

✺ Calculating risk

Our family dog of sixteen years died last night. His name was Frank. He was hit by a car.

Now, in no way do I fault the driver. Frank just walked out in front of her, as he had done on more than one occasion. He'd always been lucky before.

As I mourn the great loss to our family, I ponder this idea of calculating risk. Years ago, my husband made the decision that it was more important for Frank to have freedom to roam our neighborhood than for him to have that extra measure of protection under our continually watchful eye.

You see, Frank was not just our dog; he was the neighborhood's dog. Amazingly well known in our community (often called by name by people we had never even met!), he was nicknamed "the Mayor." There was something about how he walked as he surveyed the sidewalks that convinced us all that in spite of his short dachshund stature, he, indeed, was in charge. I get that: His freedom was an important part of his life.

But what good does that fact do me now? He has no life. Did we "win" with sixteen full years of freedom or did we "lose" with more time stolen? What is the final assessment of this calculated risk?

For sixteen years we lived on the "upside." Now we are devastated by the "downside" of that choice. Why couldn't he have died another way? In some fashion disconnected from our choice? It seems to hurt more because it is the end result of a risk we knowingly took.

I wish that I could say I am at peace with my husband's choice in spite of the current pain. But I am not. I am struggling. Is it just my pain or is there a real message, some wisdom in this unrest?

Clearly, it was my husband's decision to make. Frank was his devoted companion. In fact, he was the only one Frank ever really listened to…we used to say he was "God" to Frank. He suffers more than any of us.

There was a part of me that had feared this traumatic event for years. Though at times I offered my more risk-averse opinion, it was his decision. Though we did not share the decision, we do share the pain. Maybe that's the part I am really railing against. I chose to not protect myself. Now I hurt.

This tumor journey has been one risk calculation after another. I hate this calculating risk.

▶ What risks do you find yourself calculating these days? How do you feel about the process?

All right, God, I don't just hate calculating risk, I hate risk, period. No more loss, God, no more.

✤ Grounded by grief

I have decided that brown is actually a more appropriate color for mourning than black. In my experience, there is something about profound grief that intuitively connects me to the ground…the earth…the richness of dark brown loamy soil.

Maybe it's the physical act of grave-digging. Or the color of winter.

Grief has a way of stripping life of all the niceties…all the comforting illusions I count on every day. Things like assumptions that our dear dog, Frank, would be in our lives forever. Or that serious health problems would never threaten our children. Or that our parents, all now in their eighties, would be with us always.

Grief lands me in a very earthy, very raw place.

But there are special gifts even here. There is a solid feeling to this time for me…like sensing the rock beneath, a decidedly steady foundation. This morning as we chanted psalms of praise at the monastery, there was a depth to the meaning of those words for me that I do not always feel.

It is as if when all the fluff is stripped away, I don't find nothingness, as I feared, but instead I discover my very ground. A ground that is clear and firm and sure. A ground that holds.

There are other meanings for the word "grounded"…such as what happens to an airplane when repairs are needed…a restriction from flight. Something in that fits, too. This is not a time for dreaming, for ideas, for imagination, for flight.

This is instead a season of living with as much physical sensation as possible. For touching and tasting, seeing, smelling, and hearing all that remains. There is comfort in the concrete…it is all I can take in now. It is all I can trust. Somehow, it gives me traction and propels me toward healing even in the midst of pain that seeks to paralyze me.

Yes, brown is the color of this season for me. I believe this to be the soil of new growth for my soul as I allow myself to be grounded by grief.

▶ What thoughts or experiences help to ground you? Do you feel more or less grounded by grief and pain?

"My God, my rock, in whom I take refuge." 2 Samuel 22:3

❧ Grief and loss

Though these two words are often used together, almost synonymously, I see them as two distinct ideas…and there is a critical importance to that difference.

Loss is a hole in my life. For me today, that means the absence of our dog to lick my ice cream bowl as he has done for the last sixteen years. In the case of divorce, it can be the absence of a life partner and the sudden evaporation of all the dreams you had made with that person. In Alzheimer's, it is the absence of memory with all the relationship and history you once shared. Loss is a hole in my life.

Grief, however, is one of a multitude of choices I can make when I experience such a hole. And not the easiest choice at that. It is far more appealing to fill that hole with noise or busyness. To try to erase it with platitudes or false reassurances that "everything will be fine." At times, I simply want to deny there even is a hole. No, grief is not the easy choice.

To grieve is to feel the aching void rather than seek to fill it. To ache, to moan, outwardly or inwardly, to give in to deep-seated longing and lament. It can look like anger (anywhere along the continuum of simple frustration to rage), sadness, bargaining, or any number of emotions we generally label as "negative." Interestingly, though often experienced as a negative, grief is really the most healing option.

So, where do I begin? As I have mentioned before, there are more psalms of lament than any other kind of psalm. It's a good place to start. Ritual is important, too. Today we are planning our dog's funeral.

To choose to grieve is to let the loss penetrate my life. A hole that penetrates? An odd image, I know, but true. Even a hole, even emptiness, even a void can be engaged or avoided.

So, today, I sit with my ice cream bowl, empty before me, needing to be licked. I share the moment with my daughters. We will look at pictures and tell stories, exploring the depths of this new hole in our lives, seeking to know it better and engage it more fully. We allow the day to be filled with both grief and loss.

► What losses have you suffered in this journey? When have you chosen grief? When have you elected other options?

Heal me, O God, and I shall be healed. Save me, and I shall be saved.

❧ Re-imagining life

At this point in our tumor journey, it seems my chief task at hand is to begin to re-imagine life. We have only one investigative visit left and it will probably not change Bob's decision to watch and wait on this tumor. It is time for me to try to move on.

For most of my life, I have felt that my tendency to imagine the future was problematic. It certainly seemed to produce a lot of pain and disappointment from time to time. For instance, because I can so easily imagine (or at least guess) what my life would have been like the last few months *without* the tumor, my sense of loss and grief are larger.

Because of that imagination-initiated pain, I decided I simply wouldn't imagine at all. I would banish all thoughts regarding the future to the realm of unreliable nonsense, living only in today.

While it is admirable to live with a great awareness of the present, I was only fooling myself to think that I could exist without some idea of what coming days will offer me, even as inexact as that projection must be.

So, I begin to imagine serial MRIs, one every three months for a while. I imagine quarterly follow-up visits with the endocrinologist. Maybe we can coordinate these visits so we just make one trip to Houston…no, it will have to be two, to do the MRI, then meet the next day with the doctor once it's read. I imagine the possibility of chemo (the one option we are still investigating).

I imagine Bob once again with long or longish brown hair, no more scary scar on his head in everyday sight. I picture him sending in a deposit for a fall law school restart and applying for scholarships. I imagine him taking his time to look for a good deal on an apartment, this time one that allows dogs. Hey, maybe those extra trips to Houston will be most convenient after all.

I imagine the bills trickling in slowly, bonuses being good for my husband at work and my being able to sell this work in time to cover the needs. I imagine good scholarship money for our daughters. I imagine figuring out some way to have this tumor covered by insurance when we can no longer cover it in a few years.

By faith, I imagine goodness and abundance as I do the critical work of re-imagining life.

▶ Where are you currently in your grief journey? In free fall? Managing? Mourning? Re-imagining? Healed?

"Now faith is the assurance of things hoped for, the conviction of things not seen."
Hebrews 11:1

❧ They haven't seen the MRI

In my struggle to shift from months of crisis back to a newly defined routine, I realized today that one of my hesitancies is that it feels like no one in my world understands what a serious medical situation we are opting to live with…simply because fixing it would be even worse.

I can see why they don't understand. They haven't seen the MRI. They haven't looked at the images of shifted structures in our son's brain. They haven't seen the proximity of this intrusion to critically life-giving parts of his anatomy.

They haven't spoken with the neuro-ophthalmologist who simply could not believe her own tests…that with an MRI like our son's, he had no visual impairment. They haven't witnessed the serious faces and voices of the neurosurgeons with whom we have visited.

All they see is a young man with a shaved head and a smallish scar. A twenty-three-year-old with all his wit, humor, and mental faculties intact, albeit without much facial hair. They hear that he enjoys his job at the law firm, wins at Scrabble, loves to play poker with neighbors, and is looking forward to returning to law school next fall. And, certainly, that is a true picture—but they haven't seen the MRI.

Neither did they see him in the Intensive Care Unit that day, completely unresponsive. Neither have they felt the multiplied impact of that moment, because it is still without medical explanation. The doctors simply say, "It is a very sensitive part of the brain." Yes, and we are leaving a tumor in there?!

Am I being negative or am I realistic? Is this the alarmist nurse-mother in me over-reacting to a minimal threat or a rational and informed assessment of a very delicate and precarious situation?

I am not sure where or how I could get those questions answered. What I do know is that today I am struggling to move forward because I feel as if no one understands the difficulty of the reality we are moving into, simply because they haven't seen the MRI.

▶ What parts of your current burden or loss seem most hidden or least understood by others? Where do you feel most alone?

God, do you see? Do you understand? This is not just my imagination, is it, God? How I wish it were!

❧ Adjusting my yoke

I never know where comfort will come from on any given day. Often, it surprises me. Such was the case today. On my hour-long exercise walk with my new MP3 player, I was enjoying some music when the lyrics of one of the songs caught my attention. The songwriter made reference to

Matthew 11:28–30: "Come to me, all you that are weary and are carrying heavy burdens, and I will give you rest. Take my yoke upon you, and learn from me; for I am gentle and humble in heart, and you will find rest for your souls. For my yoke is easy, and my burden is light."

Burden bearing…my topic of the week. As I am seeking to discover some new way to live with this unexpected burden of my small piece of our son's tumor, I suddenly realized that it would help a great deal if I would spend some time adjusting the yoke.

As I have noted before, I am a very visual person. The image of being yoked with Jesus as I travel through life has always been a real comfort for me. As I imagine it, the burden bearing has never been evenly divided. In mercy, Jesus shares with me only that which I can carry. By definition, Jesus has made sure that my burdens are easy and light. When they feel otherwise, it means it's time to re-adjust the yoke.

In my years working as a hospital chaplain, I have had numerous encounters with elderly people whom I refer to as mystics. They are people who walk so closely in God's presence that listening to them speak feels like hearing the very voice of God. One such man named Tobe gave me this exhortation as I was finishing a visit one day: "Don't just lean on Jesus, young lady, learn to lean *heavy* on Jesus."

So, today, as I hear Jesus' comforting words from long ago and Tobe's wise and deep voice echo in my soul, I will choose to lean *heavy* on Jesus. I am not in this alone. I will never bear this burden alone.

Today, comfort came in the form of adjusting my yoke.

▶ Who shares your load? How good are you at letting others help? Is it time to re-adjust the yoke?

What in the world would I do without you, God?

Hating helplessness

I don't think I am alone in my hatred of helplessness. Most of us visibly cringe at even small encounters with this painful phenomenon, such as when we watch a child fall, or the car in front of us in a traffic jam suddenly stops and we cannot avoid a collision. We take great pains to protect ourselves from experiencing any degree of helplessness.

As I have sought to adjust myself to the reality of life with this tumor, I realize one of my chief struggles centers on this issue. Moving forward now means accepting life with a huge new element of helplessness.

> We do not know *how* the tumor will grow. We are helpless to stop it if it does.
>
> We do not know *where* the tumor may grow. We are helpless to direct it.
>
> We do not know *when* the tumor may grow. We are helpless to forestall it.
>
> We do not know *what* effects the tumor may have if it grows. We are helpless to predict it.

We have been told that it is miraculous that our son has so few symptoms given the size and location of the tumor. It has been said that he is undoubtedly on the verge of developing more severely disruptive physical deficits. It feels like maintaining any sense of normalcy in our lives will rely upon a perpetual miracle of God to keep this tumor at bay.

Is God up to perpetuating a miracle?

Am I up to relying on God to perpetuate a miracle?

Am I willing to live with such vulnerability?

Am I willing to live with such dependence on God?

Suddenly, I'm awake.

How dare I think that I am not dependent on God for my next breath? How dare I be so foolish as to assert my foolish and false independence by hating helplessness?

► What aspects of your journey put you most in touch with your helplessness?

God, I know you say that when I am weak, I am strong. Really? It doesn't feel that way.

❧ This new normal

I find myself actively resisting adjusting to this new normal in our lives. I am angry it is not all over by now. Fixed. Finished. Solved. Resolved. I don't want to adjust because I don't like it one bit.

The radiation oncologist we met with last week did not understand my frustration. When I said I had wanted this all tied up neatly with a bow before Christmas, she said, "Well, you almost made it," referring to the fact that we would have only one investigative appointment left for after the holidays.

She didn't get it. I wanted this thing *done*. Out. Forever gone from our lives. Off the radar screen entirely. And we are not even close to that. Not even close. It may be years. It may never be gone.

She said something else I've pondered, too. At one point in the visit, she commented to our son, "It sounds like you and this tumor have developed quite an amicable relationship."

Why do I resist that idea? It is, after all, true. Though the tumor has moved Bob's optic tract, he has no visual deficits. Though he has deficits in two of four pituitary hormones, he has the most important ones still functioning. Indeed, he has a pretty amicable relationship with this tumor.

Almost all these tumors are diagnosed in childhood because they create problems. His tumor grew so exceedingly slowly that, for the most part, his body simply accommodated it. If it were not for these subtle symptoms that even his nurse mom missed for years, we would not know about the tumor at all!

"It sounds like you and this tumor have developed quite an amicable relationship."

My hope, my prayer, is that "amicable relationship" will continue to define this new normal.

▶ Are there graces in your journey that you find hard to accept because they are not the particular graces you prefer?

Truly, God, I do not mean to be ungrateful, but I am not inclined to settle for this amicable relationship. I want healing.

❧ Still processing

It has now been a full four weeks since that terrifying day when our son could not wake up after his biopsy surgery. Yes, technically, it was really just a matter of several hours. Yes, he's absolutely fine now. Nevertheless, at 11:24 last night when I remained awake reflecting on those hours, I realized that I am still processing that frightening experience.

Part of what made that event so disruptive for me is that it confirmed my most significant fears. From the moment I finally realized that this was not just an "ordinary" pituitary tumor and began reading about its true location, I have been fearful of messing with this mysterious structure known as the hypothalamus.

Though there were other more easily defined fears such as hormone imbalance and blindness, this particular threat was both vague and significant. This was the region of the brain that they cannot fix if it is damaged. There are no medicines; there is no healing treatment. I recognized early on that this is the region that could cost Bob his life, not just his sight.

When the doctor suggested doing the biopsy from above, near the region I was most concerned about, I had an interesting reaction. Rather than voicing my fears and raising a question, I chose to defer to his expertise. He was not as concerned as I; surely he was right. In fact, I realize now that I was kind of looking forward to challenging my deepest fears, to having them invalidated by a routinely successful procedure.

Instead, in those few frightening hours, my worst fears were confirmed, almost cast in concrete.

So, what do I do now? Just engage the fear? Validate it within myself? Accept this as a substantial and ongoing vulnerability?

I would rather it go away. Why, oh why didn't it just go away?

Clearly, I am still processing.

▶ What are your greatest, yet-to-be-spoken fears in your current circumstance? What do you tend to do with your fears?

God, this trauma only validated and fueled my fears. Yet, you say, "Do not be afraid." Help me understand. Help me find that place of courage and trust.

❧ Small things

I think my heart is healing. Today, I noticed some small things for which to be thankful.

I mean really small things…like the fact that this winter my feet have not been cold. We live in an old wooden house seated on a pier-and-beam foundation. Most of the year, our weather is temperate, warm or downright *hot*, so the elevation is advantageous, keeping the house cooler. However, when our brief winter comes, our hardwood and tile floors can make my feet impossibly cold.

This year, however, I bought some boots. I intentionally bought them large enough to accommodate a pair of tights *and* a pair of socks beneath. Jenna calls them my "go-go" boots but actually they are quite fashionable, simply styled black leather. An extra plus: They are even waterproof, so our wet winters cannot penetrate this blessed haven of warm toes.

Today, I stopped to be thankful for a winter of warm feet.

I also noticed how warm the communion wine made my tummy feel. My mother-in-law had always attended a church that used grape juice for communion. When she visited our church several years back, the wine surprised her. As she raised her eyebrows in delight, she remarked, "Wooo, that really warms my tummy."

Today, I noticed how the wine warmed my tummy and was thankful.

Even as I write, there is a gentle rain falling outside my window. It's the rain of a warm front, slow and steady, descending from a bright gray, soft sky. No dark swirling clouds, lightning, or thunder, nothing threatening at all, just a soothing shower to water my pansies.

I think my heart is healing.

I have spent many days giving thanks for large things like good doctors and insurance and deferrable law school admissions and prayer partners and diagnoses of slow-growing tumors and strength and a son who woke up and comfort and the protection of optic nerves and hormones.

Today, I was especially thankful—to be thankful—for small things.

▶ Look at your own recent patterns of thanksgiving. Do they tell you anything about the state of your soul?

Every good gift comes from you, God. Thank you. The more I see, the more I feel your love.

Where God wants to be found

Father Colm said, "We have a perpetual temptation to try to find God where we want to find God rather than where God wants to be found."

I want to find God in

Serenity

Sunsets at the beach

Puppies who play

Innocence

Peaceful walks in the woods

Chocolate mousse

I don't want to find God in

Tumors

Dwindling bank accounts

Old cars

Puppies who pee on my white wool rug

Tsunamis

Anger

I know God can be found in all these places from time to time. I have seen God in these places.

God has promised that if I seek, I will find, if I seek with all my heart.

So, the real question for today is: Do I really even want to know where God wants to be found?

▶ Where do you tend to look for God? Where have you "found" God lately?

"'Come,' my heart says, 'seek his face!' Your face, Lord, do I seek." Psalm 27:8

✤ It's all in the gardener's intent

I spent yesterday pulling weeds in my garden. At the end of the day I had quite a large mound (three feet by three feet!) of a single type of weed. Now, labeling this particular plant a "weed" is probably a debatable entitlement. Though I'm not sure of its official name, it is some form of "wandering Jew." It has a narrow green leaf with a purple underside and a delicate white flower when in bloom. I have seen it intentionally planted in many gardens, draping beautifully over walls or baskets.

But, to me, it was a weed. It was drowning the small hydrangeas I transplanted last fall and threatening some well-established azaleas. Though it started small, simply as a tag-along with some plants my mother had given me, it definitely "wandered" far from its meager beginnings.

"It's all in the gardener's intent," I thought to myself. These green and purple leaves could be a lovely addition to the garden or a nuisance. It's all in the gardener's intent. And, for whatever reason, as I am prone to do, I suddenly made a connection. "It's just like fear."

Fear? Yes, fear. Struggling for months with fear, I kept trying to get a handle on it. On one hand I read in Scripture that "fear is the beginning of wisdom," a good thing. Later, I read that "perfect love casts out fear," putting fear on the other end of the spectrum. So, I have been asking, which is it?

Perhaps, as with the "wandering Jew," it can be either, depending on the gardener's intent. For most of my life, I have considered my tendency toward fear to be a bad thing. Struggling to free my life from the limitations it wants to impose has been a continual battle. Especially in seasons like this one. I want to know more of God's love. I want to be free from my fears.

In recent years, however, my spiritual director has encouraged me to begin to see fear as more than just a weed. More than once, others have told me I am "wise beyond my years." Could that be the other side of my battle with fear? Could it be that this fear I battle has actually blessed my soul? Could it be that part of the wisdom I offer here is the fruit of my fearful heart? Weeds or a lovely planting? Love-robbing emotion or birthplace of wisdom? I guess it's all in the gardener's intent.

▶ How do you regard the fear you are experiencing in this challenging season? As friend? Foe? Both?

God, could it be that owning my fear is the path to avoiding the place where my fear owns me? Even the darkness of fear is light to you.

Using winter

My choice to spend yesterday pulling weeds in the garden was a very strategic decision. It was the last day of what I jokingly call our "January thaw." Since I live in southeast Texas, you might imagine that I do not mean "thaw" in any literal sense; half the time we go all winter without even experiencing a hard freeze. In fact, it is pretty common to have several days in December or January with temperatures well into the seventies. Such has been our last week.

But change is coming. The weatherman has assured me that we will have very cold weather all next week. So, I decided, this is a good time to pull weeds. My plan is to pull up what I can and leave the rest for the harsh weather, hopeful that the exposed roots will perish in the cold.

That sounds heartless, I know, somewhat unlike my generally compassionate soul. Perhaps that difference is why I noticed yesterday the way in which I was using the harshness of winter for good, with a vision to create a better spring. Then, as noted before, for whatever reason, I made another connection: I'm doing the same work right now within my soul.

When this tumor journey began months ago, I made the decision to engage it in a new way, becoming more intentional about dealing with the pain and grief that were sure to be a part of this uninvited experience. I made choices to slow the pace of my life way down, eliminating all non-essentials. I became intentional about engaging my grief and exploring my losses. In these writings, you have witnessed much of that process and that pain.

Only now, though, do I sense myself becoming more intentional about using the harshness of this winter for good. There's something about shedding all those tears that leaves my eyes clearer. There's something about dealing with loss and actually letting go of some things that makes it easier to let go of other things. There's something about slowing down that allows me to become aware of the need to turn, to change directions in some ways.

In the cool of this week, as I wait for our last investigative doctor's appointment, I plan to clean out the attic and sort through the filing cabinet. Taking full advantage of my slower pace, my clarity of vision and my heart that is, at least temporarily, tuned to letting go, I am using winter.

▶ In what ways is your vision clearer as a result of your present suffering?

"For everything there is a season, and a time for every matter under heaven."
Ecclesiastes 3:1

The brightness of winter

The sun is out today, strong and bright on a cold winter afternoon. It is late January and near the peak of our winter. All the leaves that will be dropped this year have fallen. Brown overcomes green as the color of the woods near the monastery where I pray. The tones are simpler, gentler; a sense of rest and quiet is perceived by my eyes, ears, and soul.

There is a pathway through the woods. Today, it seems brighter than I've ever known it to be. Perhaps I've not walked it in the winter before.

Bonnie, a dear friend from Pennsylvania, was at prayer this morning. This was the first I had seen her since our tumor journey began last fall. She had followed our story and faithfully prayed with us and for us through e-mail updates. Her knowing embrace brought tears to my eyes.

She is a woman acquainted with grief. When her husband died several years ago, she mourned his leaving well. In recent years, she has worked as a hospice volunteer, unafraid to re-engage that all too familiar heartache.

Bonnie told me she was appreciative of how we had kept her so well informed. She was thankful to be included in our journey. She could tell God had been present through it all. Then she continued in a way that surprised me.

"I remember those very hard days, and they were very hard. But I remember more the closeness of God. It was as if my senses were so much more able to perceive God, so much more alive. Sometimes I long to regain that sense of how real God was to me in my grief."

The brightness of winter. When the green is stripped away, the landscape more barren, the sun shines through in unique ways. Though at first surprised by her expression of desire, I knew exactly what Bonnie was talking about. In the last week or so, I have felt as if the fog is lifting and a new clarity of vision and life is emerging. As I close my eyes and turn my face into the warm rays, I give thanks for sunshine and clarity even when they come though the brightness of winter.

▶ Do you feel the warmth of God's presence or simply the chill of winter?

"The LORD is my light and my salvation— whom shall I fear?" Psalm 27:1a

✣ Among friends

I've hesitated to write this vignette. Even though it's an important tumor journey experience, it just seemed too intimate to write. But, after all I've written, the good, the bad, and the ugly as promised, why not dare this one…after all, I am among friends aren't I?

The middle of last August, my life felt like it was in a liminal space, all ingredients in the pot, stirring and fluid but not yet jelled…a bit like homemade pudding still in process. My book was finished and being considered by a publisher, but no news yet. Two of our three children were happily off at school, with the third beginning her senior year. I had just finished working a spell as a relief chaplain and knew it would be a while before I got another call. I was in a good spot but unsure of what might be ahead on my path.

At the monastery for prayer one evening, as was my custom, I sat in my usual preferred seat, facing the large windows on the western wall. Through the window on the left, I have a long distance view of towering pines, often dancing in our steady southeasterly breeze off the Gulf. Through the window on my right, the tangled mass of woods is close up, just outside the window.

Obviously, these views are not new to me, but for some reason that particular evening, I was struck by how difficult it would be to make a way through woods like these. Unexpectedly, the question rose within me: "Is this what is ahead for me? A mass of tangled woods?" Just as quickly came the response, "Notice the sky beyond." In both views, there were distinct patches of blue sky visible through the dense foliage. Had I just received a comforting image before experiencing a coming trauma?

Now, you may not know what to do with that moment, and neither do I. That's part of why I hesitate to share it. Was it an internal premonition? A figment of my active imagination? Or the voice of God? All I know for sure is that our tumor journey began less than a week later and that the memory of the image of blue sky beyond has indeed brought me comfort.

> "I no longer call you servants, because a servant does not know his master's business. Instead, I have called you friends, for everything that I learned from my Father I have made known to you." (John 15:15)

Perhaps, just perhaps, it was simply conversation among friends.

▶ Can you recall any internal or external premonitions of pain or comfort that hinted at your current heartache?

God, though I am grateful for the comfort, I'm not sure I want to know what's ahead anymore.

🌿 Out the window

Though I can deal well with grieving people day in and day out as a hospital chaplain, when one of my children is hurting all that expertise goes right out the window.

Our son came into our bedroom last Saturday afternoon and said, "I think I'm starting to go crazy here without friends."

Though many of his good high school friends were in over the holidays, all had returned to work or school in other cities. His friends from college were five hours away in Austin. Since returning home, we had been so entangled in this tumor journey that he had neither the opportunity nor the energy to make new ones. He was, indeed, without friends.

Now, these many days later, I can actually see Bob's lament as a hopeful statement. He's coping well enough with this tumor thing now that he's moving on with his life. No longer processing as much internally, with his energy up, he's once again in pursuit of life. Sadly, that wisdom eluded me last Saturday.

When I heard his lament, I began to strategize how I could fix it. "We should make a way for him to go to Austin this weekend," I thought. Fix it quick. End the pain. Now, if I had acted on that, it might have turned out okay—not very wise in the long term, but okay. Sadly, it gets worse.

"He can't go to Austin. Gas is too expensive. It's hard on the car. His room is a mess. He has to go through the stuff I cleaned out of the attic. And he has work on Monday." Though thankfully I didn't say all that, I said enough to shut down the grief and let him know he could not lament with me around.

Ugh. I've seen it a thousand times at the hospital. I know better. But sometimes, all that training and experience go right out the window.

▶ How do you generally respond when those around you are hurting? Do you go into fixing mode? Do you sit with them in pain? Or run the other way?

Wow, God, what a mess. What a mess of a mother I am.

❧ As it comes

From the beginning of this tumor journey, my goal was to live it as it comes.

For most of my life, whenever any form of grief entered my life, I stuffed it away on the spot. I used rationalization, platitudes, intellectualization, and even praise music to run from experiencing any actual sense of loss. At thirty-five years old, I ended up with a lifetime worth of pain that had to be slowly unpacked, experienced, and healed. It was no fun.

So, as you might recall, when this journey began, I made the conscious choice to seek to make room for my grief. It was an experiment of sorts. Though I had no idea what that would look like in practice, the decision was clear. A few weeks into all this, it became clear that one way of experiencing this "as it comes" was to write.

Over these many months, I have been faithful to my experiment. I have written in fits and starts. One of the most interesting observations I have made is that the magnitude of my internal experience of events is not necessarily very connected to the import of the actual external experience. For example, a doctor's visit that might be medically routine, without any new news or impact, can throw me into a tailspin. Or at times the confirmation of bad news that I had anticipated and grieved about in advance had little impact. Go figure!

Some stories form within me close to the time the inspiring experiences actually occur, some take weeks and months to jell. Some I write easily, others I labor over. There are times when I joyfully look forward to the chance to sit and write. Then, there are times when every piddly thing must be done and every square inch of the house must be cleaned before I surrender to my chair.

But, I am learning. Along the way, at times when my internal road was especially rough and I did not write or even consent to *think*, I was conscious of my avoidance. Though I chose denial for a while, my refusal to engage did not last long. My heart is freer than I thought it could be in this moment. It feels as if my grief and pain are "clean," more easily healed, because of this odd experiment, because of the choice to live it, and for me write it, as it comes.

▶ Do you feel that you are accumulating or storing up grief and pain? Or are you able to live it as it comes?

Journey with me, God, as the God of all comfort and the Father of all compassion. I need your help.

❧ Decision by journey

It has been intriguing to observe our son's various stages of decision making along the path of this tumor journey. In the beginning, he was quite set on having surgery. He did not care what the risk might be to life or limb, vision or hormones; this thing was coming out of his head. He said with conviction: "It's not *if*, it's *when* and *how*." The journey continued....

As we listened to multiple neurosurgeons around the nation, mostly through phone consultations, we heard those risks recounted repeatedly. In the wait time between those conversations, Bob's imagination began to explore the risks more seriously. He said at dinner one night: "I've decided that the thing I would hate most about being blind would be not being able to read and not being able to drive." The journey continued....

The possibility of biopsy had been mentioned several times along the way. One local neurosurgeon said it required a craniotomy, another from Pittsburgh thought he could do it through the nose. As the risks of surgery sank in, Bob began to consider this intermediate step. When the Houston neurosurgeon mentioned an endoscopic approach from above, Bob was ready. After much discussion, he said: "Before I decide to leave this thing in there, I need to know what it is. Let's do the biopsy." The journey continued....

When the biopsy news was good, I thought this journey was winding down. I could tell life was beginning to "normalize" for Bob because he was suddenly aware that he had no local social life. This was going to be a long nine months until school began again. Beginning to imagine life and relationships moving forward with the tumor brought an unexpected discomfort. Just before our final investigative appointment, he said: "I'm getting less and less comfortable with the 'do nothing' option. It just wouldn't be fair to my future wife or kids." The journey continued....

It had taken us five months to go from the first MRI to a conversation with an expert on Bob's particular kind of tumor. With confidence, she told Bob that the likelihood that he would need treatment for this slow-growing tumor somewhere along the way was very, very great. He said: "I prefer sooner to later. I want to do radiation." The journey continues....

As I look back, I see each decision as the fruit of faithfully embracing each place along the path, a kind of cumulative insight, a steadily unfolding wisdom, a process I've come to call decision by journey.

▶ How have you engaged the reality of gradually unfolding information and decision making?

God, I prefer efficiency and full disclosure to this unfolding journey plan. How can I know what I don't know? This is so scary.

❧ Accumulation

My life feels uncomfortably full right now. It seems to me that many kinds of accumulation in my life are connected and, for the moment, somewhat out of control. My life is tick-full from accumulated stress, mess, pounds, and wisdom.

Now the stress is understandable but I am surprised at the increased level I found myself dealing with recently. For weeks, it seemed as if this tumor journey was winding down. Bob appeared comfortable with the "do nothing for now" option. The visits were nearly completed. But as he made known his choice to pursue radiation and we turned another corner opening a new door, I have been amazed at my inability to cope the last few days. I am full of stress.

Over the weekend, I did the short-attention span stress thing, and the house quickly became a wreck. If it weren't for the fact that my husband becomes super-helpful when he is stressed, the groceries wouldn't even be bought. The very space I need to best process stress eludes me. My sense of fullness is compounded by my surroundings.

And my waistline. I was in such good shape before all this hit, and so determined not to abandon my healthy routine but, alas, the pounds are back. Why is it that I prefer to eat my emotions than to feel them? Bad habits are hard to break.

Stress, mess, pounds, and…wisdom? I have even stopped writing in the last week or so. I feel myself accumulating moments of goodness and wisdom along with everything else. This is the first time I've written in almost two weeks. Why do I avoid even goodness? Why do I spin? Why do I accumulate?

Perhaps I am afraid to let go—of anything. Perhaps I am storing my resources. Perhaps I am afraid to move forward in any arena. Maybe my fear of these radiation treatments has been translated into my fear of dealing in a productive way with my stress, house, and emotions. I want to backpedal in life.

It doesn't work. Life, including this tumor journey, moves forward with or without me. Perhaps these words evidence my acceptance of that, my choice to let go and move away from my uncomfortably full sense of accumulation.

▶ In times of stress, what kinds of things do you tend to accumulate or hoard? What do you off-load or from what do you fast?

God, today I sense your boundless patience with me and your deep well of tender compassion toward me. Thanks. I needed that.

❧ Gentle timing

The gentleness of God is one of those things I see much better in hind-sight. It is something I greatly value, especially since one of my chief fears is that of being overwhelmed by life. Gaining confidence in this aspect of God's work is a significant point of comfort for me.

A year before our tumor journey began, I was working part time as a hospital chaplain. Though I longed for more time and energy to explore a newfound giftedness and passion for writing, I was hesitant to give up the job. While I enjoyed the steady paycheck, the real reason I would not quit was the great needs of the patients and families combined with the understaffed condition of our department.

So, God "trumped" my concerns by bringing in a new departmental director who did not believe in part-time employees. "Poof." The job I was hesitant to leave left me! I was shocked. Interestingly, on my last day at work, I noticed that a story I had submitted months before to a corporate publication of the hospital's parent company was being featured on their Web site. It was as if God had ordained this segue from chaplaincy to writing, making it a gentle transition after all.

The next nine months were filled with the writing of my first book, a delightful experience for me. Amazingly, I found a publisher who offered me a contract after a relatively short search. The one disappointment was that the book had to get in a queue with other releases, delaying its publication until eighteen months from the date we signed the contract.

Enter our tumor journey. Suddenly, the delay that looked like a disappointment became a blessing. Free from the need for immediate editing, I had time for this unexpected intrusion. Gentle timing indeed.

The title of this particular vignette came to me weeks ago as I began to think this journey was ending. I thought the final "proof" of God's gentle timing would be the fact that our investigation was concluding just as my scheduled time with an editor was to begin. *Not so.*

Rather than enjoying another proof of God's gentle timing, I now have an opportunity to exercise faith. By faith, I will assume this next phase of our journey, with all its impossible-to-anticipate ups and downs, will eventually become yet another evidence of God's gentle timing.

▶ Can you see any evidence of God's gentleness in your present journey?

Open my heart, God. I want to feel the gentleness of your touch.

✥ Just enough fear

Our older daughter, Jenna, flew to Africa last Sunday. Now, taking part in a study abroad program was our idea, her choice of Africa was not. I was picturing France or Italy or England!

She began planning this venture almost a year ago. When the tumor journey entered our lives, it was tempting to ask her to not go. Both our pocketbook and emotional capacity seemed way too stressed for such a venture. Yet, it was clear to both my husband and me that this was an important trip for her, a worthy investment even in these tough times.

For months and months, she has been busily preparing: acquiring a passport, visa, shots, and knowledge about this foreign land she would be visiting. She was fully packed three weeks before she actually left. She appeared utterly confident.

About a week before she left, Jenna began to doubt herself. Fears about being able to adjust well to time differences and new foods began to surface. It did not help that she had contracted a cold from her sister and was feeling poorly for the long flight. She was very tearful as we said our goodbyes at the airport. Needless to say, so were we.

As I said many prayers for her in the hours that followed our parting, I thought again about fear. A part of me was actually thankful that she was afraid; it was evidence that she was taking this venture seriously and would be appropriately cautious in unfamiliar surroundings. "Fear is the beginning of wisdom."

I was also grateful though that her fear had not paralyzed her. She felt a calling to this experience and moved forward in the midst of her fear. "Perfect love casts out fear."

I feel the same way about Bob's decision for radiation. I have come to see that he does, indeed, take seriously the potential negative side effects of choosing treatment. There is an appropriate fear, a wise caution.

But there is also much freedom for the future to be gained by dealing with this now. His concern is for those he is yet to love and care for...a visionary and very hopeful concern. A loving decision. I think he has just enough fear.

▶ Do you experience fear in balance? When you tip, do you tend toward one side or the other? What wisdom is lost in that imbalance?

God, you are the source of wisdom. You see what I cannot. Help. Guide. O, God, protect; please, God, protect us all.

✤ Ramping up

After weeks of winding down, I am now trying to ramp up for this next phase of our tumor journey.

As I wrote earlier, my first response to Bob's decision was to move into my over-stressed spinning mode. Lots of Internet research; lots of unconscious eating; lots of under-the-surface processing. Thankfully, that did not last long, really only a weekend.

With the energy of the anxiety of the initial diagnosis long gone, I wondered if I would have what it takes to sustain movement forward. I had let go of so much energy as I had begun to allow myself to wind down. Could I find more? Where? How?

As I let go of the spinning last week, all I can say is that what I needed was there. With my feet on the ground once again, I am moving forward.

Somehow, it feels different this time. Though I have struggled for days to figure a good way to put it into words, the best I can come up with for now is that this time I feel more human.

There is a calm to this season of ramping up that was not true of the beginning of this journey. As I move forward, I breathe deeply rather than shallowly and tensely. My internal muscles and joints that will energize this venture feel warm and supple rather than stiff or cold. My mind feels alert but not panicked, processing efficiently but not racing.

When I encounter an obstacle in front of me, like a snowstorm in Boston that has me leaving messages on an unattended machine for a full week, I plod on faithfully. When I am shuffled from one department to another over the course of an entire day, ending up where I began, I am simply grateful the storm is over and there is someone on the other end of the phone. When my editor says we will be delayed in working on my book together until March and April, the months we anticipate actually doing this radiation therapy, I am somehow inclined to trust even that timing.

I do not tend to panic. I do not lose my breath. I am not feeling weary, overwhelmed, or afraid. There is a deep rhythm, a holy pace that feels like a vibrant, blood-red, healthy human heart beating with strength and goodness as I continue ramping up.

▶ How would you describe the energy that is currently moving you forward? Strength? Panic? Anger? Vision? Free-floating anxiety?

"My flesh and my heart may fail, but God is the strength of my heart."
Psalm 73:26

❧ Remembered moments

I love those mugs that say, "We do not remember days, we remember moments" (Cesare Pavese). Though I've never been quite sure if it is a memory issue or a soul issue, I know that saying rings true for me.

This book is a record of moments more than days…healing moments that come in many and various shapes and forms. There are a few of those moments that stick in my mind that haven't yet made it into a vignette. I offer them now as a random assortment.

> A quiet evening, one of many really, spent playing Scrabble and making s'mores from extra thick Hershey bars and marshmallows melted over hot coals in our fireplace. (By the way, I won the game that night.)

> The moment Bob first held his new six-week-old pug puppy. Gary instantly relaxed in his papa's arms as if he'd known him forever, as if this relationship had existed from time eternal. Bob said simply, "I couldn't be happier."

> Lunch at Hugo's, a wonderfully authentic Mexican restaurant, on one of our doctor appointment trips. The crab cakes, corn pudding, grilled asparagus, and mango sauce were so good that they brought tears to Jenna's eyes.

> The moment we spotted the "WELCOME GARY" sign on the Matthews' door. They were Gary's "second" set of parents, and Bob had carefully chosen them to care for his new pug while he was in the hospital for the biopsy. He also brought a full page of detailed instructions.

> Taking Jenna's order for crème brûlée over the cell phone when she called during our splurge dinner at Ruth's Chris Steak House the night before Bob's biopsy. For just a bit, we were all together.

> Playing a new card game in the ICU waiting room with two of Bob's friends who had driven in from Austin the day after his bi-

opsy. They were giving him time to rest and were willing to stick around to visit more.

Our friend Dr. Charles' repeated proclamation that Bob's diagnosis of a very slow-growing tumor was his favorite Christmas present this year.

Distinct and sensual, precious and healing remembered moments.

▶ What healing moments can you recall? Remember, any moment that brings a touch of goodness counts.

"I believe that I shall see the goodness of the Lord in the land of the living." Psalm 27:13

🌿 Not just on the runway

Core spiritual lessons in my life are often tied to specific experiences. It is funny how the memory of those experiences will sometimes surface at the very moment my soul needs to be reminded of a lesson now forgotten.

That very thing happened last week as I was sitting quietly in the chapel at the monastery. My mind was drifting somewhere between thoughtful planning, free-floating anxiety and prayer. Bob had decided the week before that he wanted to pursue radiation. I was beginning to actively investigate our options, specifically proton beam radiation, a more focused form of radiation available in only three locations nationwide.

In the midst of all the thoughtful planning, free-floating anxiety and prayer, a memory surfaced. One January more than a decade ago, my husband and I were passengers on a small jet landing in Austin in the middle of the night in the middle of a thunderstorm. The scene was just like something you might have seen at the movies: lightning flashing constantly outside the windows, the plane rocking back and forth in unstable winds, booms of thunder surrounding us on all sides.

To say that I was praying in that moment would be a gross understatement. With three little children at home and my husband and I in peril on this ten-seater jet, I was begging God to spare our lives. Suddenly, I realized that God was not just on the runway; God was in the plane with me.

Now, that insight might not sound very profound to you, but it was for me. For whatever reason, I tend to distance myself from God by making God a "last resort" kind of God. I put God on the runway of my life, there to do a last-minute rescue mission rather than hold and comfort me in the plane or along the way. In that moment years ago, that sudden realization allowed my soul to rest in the arms of God as we miraculously landed safely. Even the usually calm, cool pilot was still shaking as we exited the plane!

Last week, on that particularly painful day in the chapel, I needed such a reminder. Through that memory, God gently revealed to me that I was shutting God out of my thoughtful planning, free-floating anxiety, and even out of my future-focused prayer. I had forgotten that God's healing presence and comfort were available to me in this moment, that God longed to be invited into the plane with me, not just on the runway.

▶ Do you feel God's intimate comforting presence in this moment in your heart or is God more your "go to" on the runway, crisis-management Savior?

How forgetful I am, God, of how very much you love me. You are as close as my very breath.

❧ Behold the wisdom of youth

As we send out our periodic e-mail updates to friends and family who are praying for Bob, I am often encouraged by the responses we receive. Whether it is a simple "Still praying" or a "Thanks for the update," I know our message has been received with love.

When I sent out the news of Bob's decision to pursue radiation treatment for his tumor out of concern for his future spouse and family, I got an interesting response from a wise friend, Bonnie.

She began by recounting her grandson's recent skiing accident. As a result of that venture gone awry, he was now in need of extensive dental intervention to restore his youthful smile. Away at boarding school in a small town, he'd chosen to follow through with treatment there to expedite the process.

She went on to explain that as a concerned grandmother, at first she wanted to intervene, facilitating more advanced and specialized medical treatment in the large city in which she lives. Yet as she contemplated his choice alongside our e-mail about Bob's decision, she began to see things differently.

As she so aptly put it, "The young are teaching us to deal with today's troubles so that we can live more fully tomorrow—I appreciate being reminded of that!"

Thanks, Bonnie. I needed that reminder, too. It has been difficult to think about my future in the midst of this tumor journey. Next year, Lord willing, all three of our children will be away at school. For the first time in twenty-four years, I will have no kids to care for.

Before all this began, I had been looking at doctoral programs. Maybe it's time to begin looking again as I behold the wisdom of youth.

▶ Do you also have stories of hearing God's wisdom from those younger than you?

"...and a little child shall lead them." Isaiah 11:6

Not just a business transaction

We've spent a large part of the afternoon waiting for a doctor from Boston to call. Now, I'm not complaining. This is a free consultation and I was amazed that his secretary would even narrow the potential call times at all, much less to the span of a mere three hours.

As I have waited, I have become aware of how odd this feels to me. On one level, I suppose it could be seen as a business transaction. He has a service. We have a matching need.

But is any such transaction ever really simply business? We are about to encounter a person we've never met before. We know a few things about him—his education, some articles he's written. We've even seen a picture on the Web. We know where he works and what he does for a living. But there's so much more we don't know.

Is he married? Was his wife nice to him this morning? Does he have children? Is he worried about them? Does he like his job? Is he kind? What has his day been like? Busy? Satisfying? Frustrating? Did he spend a long time with Bob's films or mere moments? Did he notice that Bob is twenty-three, that he was in law school?

I guess it works both ways, though. He knows little about us. We are from Texas. Our son had a suprasellar JPA. We've chosen radiation. Maybe he'll guess from the summary we included that we are fairly educated and somewhat organized. Does he know that both my husband and Bob took the afternoon off to wait for his call? Would he care?

As a medical professional myself, I know it is sometimes hard to stay mindful of just how very human this medical "industry" really is, and always will be. The patient in 302 with the bad gallbladder is someone's dad. He has a history, a future, feelings, dreams, and fears. So does each and every person caring for him. Therein lies the real challenge. Therein lies the real satisfaction. Therein lies the transaction that matters most.

So, as I wait, I look forward to more information, more help, perhaps a new direction. But I also look forward with curiosity to the man I will meet over the phone, to what this human encounter will bring into to my life, to what I can offer him even in the midst of a myriad of medical questions. Yes, indeed, this call is not just a business transaction.

▶ As you reflect on the lives of those helping you during this hard time, do you see their human side beyond their assistance?

God, help me see as you see. I don't want to miss even one face I encounter on this journey.

❧ Hope floats

I borrowed this title from a movie that was popular a few years back. It creates for me such a vivid image of a truth I believe very strongly: God has built into our souls a lovely, sustaining penchant for hope. Hope floats.

Today, I have been thinking about how small and odd evidences of hope can be sometimes. Here are a few I've noticed along our tumor journey.

Saving the info on our trip to England rather than tossing it in the trash.

Blue sky beyond the dense woods.

Hours of Internet research, looking for a better option.

Bob filing a FAFSA (financial aid form for law school) in January.

Executing a planned study-abroad semester in Africa for Jenna.

Pursuing a second opinion.

Bob's decision to treat this tumor now for the benefit of a future spouse and children.

Inquiring about Ph.D. programs.

A beautiful pendant to remind me to look for coming moments of beauty.

Enjoying the enthusiastic greeting of a puppy whose entire body shakes with excitement when his "papa" gets home.

Bob's choice to drive two hours to a newcomer's class at a Houston church in anticipation of attending that church upon return to law school.

A family ritual of a lovely lunch or dinner after each doctor's visit.

A willingness to delay treatment two weeks to allow for Bob's vacation with friends.

Hope floats.

▶ Notice and name moments that evidence a hope beyond your current pain.

God of all hope, sustain me on this journey.

❧ Why don't I care?

A few days ago, our pastor, Logan, announced that he is resigning his position to take a job with an insurance company. Why is it that I simply don't care?

There are lots of reasons why I should care. This is quite a blow to our church, this being the fourth priest we have lost in the last several years…all for different, unrelated reasons. My husband and I are very involved in this faith community and usually hurt a great deal over events such as this.

I was also on the search committee that brought him here. The nine of us have a special investment…not to mention this was our second round after the first priest we called lasted less than a year.

And Logan is such a good priest. He has brought much healing and stability to our community. He is an outstanding preacher. He brought Bob dark beer and a book on the Trinity when he was first diagnosed. He was with us during the biopsy. And he has a lovely family. All will be missed.

So, why don't I care? Why am I so unmoved, neither grieved nor angry?

Is my emotional plate just too full?

Have I distanced myself so much during this tumor journey, trying to process it all, that I no longer really feel with my community?

Have I grown up enough to realize that life will go on?

Am I just tired of hurting over priests who disappoint me?

Am I just deferring the pain for later?

Am I ashamed, fearing we made a poor choice, unable to face myself?

Has the serious medical condition of my son shifted my priorities so completely?

Do I simply trust this good man enough to trust his decision without the need to question?

Has my faith grown to the point that I know all will be well?

Why don't I care?

▶ Describe instances where your internal responses have surprised you. What has shifted for you?

God, something in me knows this is not normal. God, why don't I care?

❧ A sense of calling

The year before this tumor journey began was a year of transition for me. I left hospital chaplaincy and began to write. As I followed what at first was an experiment, I encountered many affirmations. Some were as small as incidental remarks from fellow committee members: "You are such a wordsmith." Others were big...like a publisher agreeing to publish my book.

Alongside those affirmations, I also wrote a personal mission statement for the first time. Or, better said, it came to me. For years, I had labored over trying to formulate words that would reflect and contain my various passions. I knew friends whose lives were wisely guided by theirs and saw the wisdom in that practice; I just never could come up with one that fit me.

One Sunday morning as I was getting dressed for church, boom, it came to me, fully formed, seemingly from out of nowhere. "I am a gentle healer. I am called to invite women to a new experience of God's love and a healthier sense of self through the retelling of the stories of women in Scripture alongside the retelling of their own stories." A bit wordy, I know, but a clear direction nonetheless. It felt like the sum of all my parts.

As I finished my first book on that topic, a Bible study for women that looked at those old stories, I saw a call for workshop proposals for a conference in California. The topic was domestic violence in the church. With a soon-to-be-published book full of affirming and healing messages for women from Scripture stories, I felt that my subject matter would be especially helpful to that audience. I sent a proposal in as a long shot. Months later, I got a letter that my proposal had been accepted. Yet, I had no idea whether to accept the invitation or not.

This week, as we finally settled on a plan for radiation in Boston, I knew the calendar would allow the trip. But would I?

I need to make a decision. I need to buy my ticket. There are lots of reasons not to go: little money, fading emotional energy, performance anxiety, anticipation of being away this spring. But only one reason to go: a sense of calling.

► Has your current painful journey changed or challenged any previous sense of calling?

God, clearly my life is bigger than this crisis, so why is it so hard to engage and move forward with the non-crisis parts? You would think I would welcome the distraction!

❧ Big rooms are made for dancing

Dreams are a very biblical form of hearing from God, but I often hesitate to put much stock in them, especially when I first have a new one. Over the years, however, they have been helpful to me. Not so much as a way of predicting the future but more so as a way of helping me identify parts of my current experience that I am having a difficult time acknowledging or naming.

A few weeks ago, I had a dream of a large room, filled with soft yellow sunlight. The creamy white walls and the golden wood floors beautifully reflected the light that streamed in from a full, two-story-high wall of paned windows. The room was empty except for me. And I was dancing with great grace and freedom, inspired by and thoroughly enjoying the large open space. Though I did not understand the dream completely, the core message was clear: Big rooms are made for dancing. I somehow knew I needed to hold on to that image. Toward that end, I changed my e-mail password to "dancefloor."

That dream came back to me this week as I pondered my struggle over buying that plane ticket to California. I could not unpack my hesitancy. In fact, there were three events in my future that I was feeling the same anxiety around: the California conference, the temporary move to

Boston for our son's radiation treatment, and a book promotion trip to Nashville I had hoped to make in May. Unsure of the connection, I took a morning and found some quiet at the monastery.

Over the course of a morning spent with Scripture, watercolors, and prayer, I realized that all those ventures felt like very big rooms to me, open space, unfamiliar, frightening in their size. I felt very, very small. Taking my healing message for women and the search for healing for our son to a national level somehow felt like reaching beyond some invisible barrier previously set up in my life. Perhaps I was moving beyond what my parents could ever do or imagine, and it felt like virgin territory. Whatever the source of my hesitancy, that's when I remembered my dream. Because of that sleeping vision months before, I knew that big rooms did not have to be frightening, they could be inspiring and enjoyable; they could be spaces filled with dancing.

Later that day, my good friend John showed my husband and me a program he had taped from the Travel Channel this past week: Boston in high definition! As a native Bostonian, he was so excited about facilitating our trip, about sharing the beauty of his city. In his enthusiasm, I heard again the comforting, inspiring, and exciting invitation from God: Big rooms are made for dancing.

▶ Have you had any helpful or comforting dreams in this journey? Have you encountered any "big rooms," places unfamiliar to you, beyond your usual boundaries of place, thought, or experience?

God, I feel you expanding my soul. I am glad you also seem to know how frightening that is for me. The comfort is much appreciated.

⁊ꝛ Rubbish floats, too

As I wrote a while back, hope floats. But this week is not about hope, but about the fact that rubbish floats, too. I love the images used by the authors of Scripture that help us grasp the ways and work of God. One such image is that of the refining process. As precious metals are purified over fire; the heat allows the rubbish to float. God uses tough times to purify our lives.

I recognized that truth anew this week when I came face to face with a rather large piece of long-avoided rubbish in my life: my relationship with money. Under the heat of our tumor journey, it has risen to the top and I sense that God is inviting me to finally deal with it.

This piece of trash has been floating to the surface for a while now. Last summer, a friend challenged me on my hesitancy to charge for the spiritual direction I offer several clients. Our conversation exposed just how afraid I am to deal with money.

Then our tumor journey began. Though certainly my primary concern has been for our son's health, money has been a clear secondary anxiety. Making the decision to go to Boston is easy. If spending six weeks in Boston lowers the risk to his vision and brain, we go. Though the decision is easy, figuring out how to pay for it will not be. The very thought brings forth unimaginably large amounts of anxiety for me.

I have such poor judgment when it comes to money, so my default is to be super frugal, to the point of being miserable and making others miserable, too. I have such moral anxiety about debt that I cannot see what is loving and responsible and what is not.

When I think about Boston, all I think about are the many decisions to be made around money: where to stay, where to eat, would it be okay with God if we went to a ballgame at Fenway Park or out to eat at an oyster bar? How about a side trip to see friends in Vermont? Where is the line?

That really is the crux of the issue: I want to be faithful but don't know what faithfulness with money looks like. I've heard it said that Jesus talks more about money than almost anything else. It is curious that I've never taken a comprehensive look at what he says. I guess now is my chance because rubbish floats, too.

▶ What rubbish in your life has floated to the top in the midst of this hard time? How are you dealing with it?

"Have mercy on me, O God, according to your steadfast love; according to your abundant mercy blot out my transgressions." Psalm 51:1

✤ Growth spurts

I am beginning to notice an interesting rhythm in this tumor journey. It seems like it has been a series of external shifts followed by internal adjustments I like to think of as growth spurts. The external shifts are things like new information (operable/not operable), new experiences (the biopsy drama/trauma), or new decisions (no treatment/ treatment).

The internal shifts or growth spurts come where those particular events intersect the growing edge of my life. For instance, the "big room fear thing" was something I was learning as a part of growing into my calling, but anticipating this trip to Boston was definitely a part of what spurred me to confront that issue.

The money thing is another example. It is an issue I've struggled with my entire adult life, almost like gnats constantly flying around my head. Needing all my resources for the tumor journey rather than giving some to the annoying gnats has spurred me on to finally deal with them.

Yet other examples are the unconscious eating thing or the stall tactics I've historically used to deal with issues of grief and loss in my life.

One of the graces of this journey has been the gentle pace with which it has unfolded. The incremental nature has allowed me the privilege of making these internal shifts as the external shifts arise. I know that others in crisis might not have that same opportunity.

All that having been said, in the midst of gratitude for the pace and growth, I must confess that I would still prefer for God to create a different way, all right, a less painful and frightening way, for me to experience growth spurts.

▶ What new growth have you noticed in your own life and soul since this painful passage began? Are there any patterns you can observe?

"So that you may lead lives worthy of the Lord, fully pleasing to him, as you bear fruit in every good work and as you grow in the knowledge of God." Colossians 1:10

❧ Just a hoax

We are six months into this journey and I have to admit there are still times when I just want it to go away.

The other day, I thought, "What if it's all just a hoax?"

I remember all the speculation around the first moonwalk. There were conspiracy theories that contended that it was all a hoax, that the images were created somewhere here on earth. Some said it was the ultimate governmental scam. After all, we ordinary folk never really had any verifiable proof to the contrary.

The same could be said for Bob's tumor. It's tucked so far in the middle of his head that we certainly can't see it. The only one who has seen it is the same "expert" who reads the images and says there's something there.

Bob looks okay (except for the lack of a beard). He feels fine. Maybe it's just a hoax.

Now, I'm not so crazy as to believe in moments such as these. I am very surprised that this far down the road, denial would be such a temptation. How nice it would be to forget all this and just pretend.

Unfortunately—or better said, fortunately—reason brings me down to earth and I move forward. I am comforted by the fact that just as I believe in this invisible tumor, I also believe in an invisible God.

This is not just a hoax.

▶ Have you been tempted by denial? What aspects of this journey seem the easiest to ignore?

God, I think perhaps I am in more pain than I would like to admit.

✣ Struggling

Tonight we went to the monastery for Evening Prayer. I had been looking online all afternoon for affordable places to stay in downtown Boston. I've concluded that that's an oxymoron…those two things are contradictory: Boston and affordable housing.

To be fair, none of these tumor journey expenses were in our long- or short-range spending plan. So, actually, nothing seemed affordable to me. What was the difference between $89 a night and $139 a night when you really couldn't afford any of it! To say the least, I was struggling. And very much looking forward to Evening Prayer as a remedy for that struggle.

Many times I have come to this particular time and rhythm of prayer feeling heavily burdened. In the words of chanted psalms, in hymns and songs of God's faithfulness such as Mary's Song or Zechariah's Song and in silence, I have found comfort, relief, and release. At the end of the service, the final "Amen" often echoes for me a new level of acceptance for the struggle of the day, an internal sense of "So be it."

Not so tonight. In fact, I was struck by just the opposite reality. Though I generally wrestle a bit with trying to free my thoughts from concerns of the day, today it was a struggle I just could not win. At the end of the twenty minutes of silence, I was in just as much turmoil as when I began. There was a notable absence of that longed for "Amen" of the soul.

I felt ashamed of my anxiety, my fear, my lack of faith in the goodness and providence of God. I felt stuck and a bit hopeless. I felt caught in a prison of my own making, unable to free myself. I felt "help less" in every sense of those words.

As we moved from the chapel to the monastery to share a bit of dinner with our friends, I carried my anxiety, despair and shame.

The first thing John said to me that evening was, "Tia has asked me to approach you guys about whether it would be okay with you if we tried to raise some money for you to help with extra expenses in Boston."

God heard my cry and rescued me. God parted the waters and freed me, coming to me in the flesh, in the body of Christ. God saw me, loved me, had compassion on me, and did not shame me for struggling.

▶ How has God met you in your struggle along the way? Has God parted the waters for you?

"The Lord is my strength and my might, and he has become my salvation."
Exodus 15:2

❧ Tired of being sad

I decided the other night that I was just flat tired of being sad.

I had spent the weekend as a delegate to our diocesan council. It looks likely that the Episcopal Church as I now know it will not be around as that unified body much longer. Issues have arisen that are too deep and too large. They overwhelm our desire for unity. I was sad as I thought about future councils with huge chunks of our particular body not present.

To magnify it all, I sat next to my priest and friend, Logan, who will be leaving next week. It was the first time I had really been able to visit with him since the announcement of his resignation. I will miss his sermons, his presence at the altar, and his friendship. I am sad to see him go.

There were several folks at council that I had not seen in the course of the last year. As we visited, naturally, I told them, usually with tears, about this tumor journey. They faithfully shared my grief, affirming the pain of such an unexpected life intrusion. Coming from every angle, the whole weekend seemed covered by a heavy blanket of sadness.

When I got home, I told my husband of my experience and suggested that we go find a romantic comedy at the video store for some relief. We found three and I picked one at random. It was *Raising Helen*. Now, if you've seen the movie, you know what's coming next.

Technically, it is a romantic comedy. And a pretty good one at that. However, the plot of the movie centers on Helen's growth into motherhood after accepting the guardianship of her sister's three children upon the sudden death of their parents. What could be sadder than the grief of three small children!

"Uncle!" I cried out to God that night. It felt like a divine set-up. There was no escape even if I was tired of being sad.

▶ As you continue to walk this journey, what points of fatigue have you experienced? What has fostered resilience in you? What has brought despair?

Renew my strength, O God. I am beyond my own.

❧ Feeling sorry for yourself

As I sat in church yesterday, I suddenly realized that I was feeling very sorry for myself.

Woe is me. This tumor journey is hard work. Researching the tumor, researching treatments, doctor visits, insurance forms, insurance replies, insurance appeals, and bills. Add to that researching life in another city: housing, churches, contacts, mass transit, flights, cell phones. Saving all our receipts, receipts, receipts. Not to mention a whole new medical system to explore. Woe is me.

Woe is me. This tumor journey feels like such an interruption in my personal journey. I had barely gotten on the way toward finally living into my calling when I got knocked off that path. It had taken me so long to even figure out what I was to do…and now, another delay. When will I have the time and energy to return to my passion? Woe is me.

Woe is me. My pastor is leaving. How could he leave now? It couldn't be worse timing for me personally. Though I know the world doesn't revolve around me, that doesn't mean I can't still acknowledge that this is especially painful timing. Woe is me.

Woe is me.

All my life I've been told: "Feeling sorry for yourself never helped anyone."

I beg to differ. Who better to feel sorry for me than me? Who else knows the full extent of my personal experience of pain? I know "me" from the inside out.

And, if I don't extend compassion toward myself and my own pain, will I really ever be able to extend it to others?

"Feeling sorry for yourself never helped anyone." I beg to differ.

Perhaps that sentiment came from someone who did not understand the healing potential of grief. Perhaps they did not know it is a journey, not a destination.

Woe is me. Sometimes, healing begins with unabashedly and unapologetically feeling sorry for yourself.

▶ How do you feel about feeling sorry for yourself? Have you found it to be helpful or not?

God, you comfort me with a comfort I can later give to others. Today, though, it's all about the receiving end of that equation; it's all about me.

❧ Faithfulness and rest

One of the most difficult things for me to fathom in the Christian life is the relationship between faithfulness and rest.

> *"In returning and rest you shall be saved.*
> *In quietness and trust shall be your strength." Isaiah 30:15*

I come from a long line of "doers." So, it is no surprise, that I generally define faithfulness to God in terms of doing. This rest and trust thing just doesn't come easily for me. On some level I do, however, understand that in my insistence on "doing" I often end up acting as if there is no God. I've also noticed that the more I "do," the more alone I feel. God is inviting me to repentance, to live a new way.

Faithfulness can also be defined as…

accepting my human limitations, my need for space and rest, privacy and moments of beauty.

freeing myself from ministry commitments to allow time to live this tumor journey as it unfolds.

following doctor appointments with a nice lunch or dinner.

taking time to redeem the massage certificate my kids gave me for Christmas even before I find a place to live in Boston.

accepting the financial help of willing friends; embracing the reality that some things in life are not meant to be borne alone.

leaving town for a weekend to publicize my book even though I'll soon be gone for seven weeks in a row.

daring to enjoy the freedom and (gasp) *delight* of being in Boston!

I look forward to learning more about this oddly shaped repentance, this strange relationship between faithfulness and rest.

▶ Do you tend to define faithfulness in terms of doing only? What might faithfulness as rest look like in your journey?

Could it be, God, that you are this good and this kind...to me?

❧ A community of stories

Episcopalians are creatures of habit. We love our liturgy and our chosen seats. I tend to sit about seven-eighths of the way toward the back, all the way to the outside edge of the right-hand wall.

I like that pew for two reasons. First, it has an awesome view of the towering trees that cover the expansive lawn outside our nave as well as the prayer garden. In the spring when the azaleas and dogwoods bloom, it is undeniably the best seat in the house.

The other reason I like that spot is that as the minister preaches, I can see almost the entire congregation (since he stands in a pulpit on the left side of the nave.) As I hear God's Word expounded, I look around at the people whose lives have been shaped by that Word. I remember their stories of brokenness and recall their stories of healing. We are indeed a community of stories. Stories of healing like

...a woman whose college-age daughter died suddenly in an unexplained accident. She is now leading a grief group.

...a marriage torn by unfaithfulness, now mended and growing.

...an elderly doctor who fell off a fence while ranching with his grandsons, endured two craniotomies even as a cardiac patient, and now bakes bread and delivers it to each and every person who visits our church.

...a mother with a recent multiple sclerosis diagnosis who is exceedingly thankful for the strength to keep working at a job she enjoys.

There are also stories that need healing like...

...the couple married over fifty years who just received devastating news of his pancreatic cancer diagnosis.

...the young mother whose husband is now in Iraq.

...our son.

I smile to myself. I have found new comfort and hope today by sitting in the midst of a community of stories.

▶ Whose story do you know that gives you comfort on this journey?

God, today I give thanks for your faithfulness to heal others; and I hope for the same for us.

✣ Healing creativity

The preacher reminded me the other night that evil can never create, only attempt to distort and deform. Only God can create.

One of the intriguing aspects of this tumor journey has been the healing I have experienced through writing. To some extent, I think that healing comes from simply journaling, putting thoughts on paper, getting them out of my head and onto the page in such a way that they seem more manageable. The act of writing can be purifying and purging in a healthy way.

But, that is not all that is contained in these vignettes. There has also been an aspect of merging my particular life wisdom with my current experience. Though those connections could be a forced thing, as the different topics have floated to the surface, the joining of the two has felt very unforced, organic, in the flow of living and coping with life. In these pages, I have often "said" to myself many of the things I have said to others in years of working as a chaplain. That merging of recorded experience and wisdom is especially healing.

So, there's journaling plus wisdom, but I think perhaps there is yet another piece to this process that has added yet another dimension of healing: creativity. As I seek to shape words around all the swirling facts and ideas in such a way as to communicate and engage the reader, I am using my particular giftedness and calling to create something larger than the simple sum of the parts. Through God's grace, I am engaged in a new, creative work. Within that creative process, I experience still more of the healing presence of God.

I happen to believe that there is no such thing as a human being who is not creative. It is a part of our birthright as those created in the image of God. Many people, however, have not discovered or recognized their particular medium for their particular expression of creativity. For me, that's writing. For another it may be creating a Sunday school curriculum or arranging flowers, repairing cars or leading small groups. I have seen a divorcée healed as she pulled weeds and planted a garden. I have witnessed marvelous displays of creativity in home decoration, sewing, pastoral visitation, and teaching. The list of possibilities is as varied as our fingerprints but one thing is constant: the Presence of God abides in healing creativity.

▶ What creative endeavors do you enjoy? Have you engaged them lately? Have they brought any comfort, insight, or healing?

O, God, thank you for this good work that you have given me to do...and the healing it brings to my soul.

🌿 Goodness and abundance

I am still struggling to learn how to expect and experience goodness and abundance from God in the physical realm. Though there are many people I know who live wisely, generously, graciously, and at peace with wealth, I struggle with physical blessings. Perhaps it is my past, perhaps it is my personality, but I am not sure how to understand this aspect of God.

I "get" justice issues and the saving mercy of God. But just how broadly do the benefits of grace extend beyond this "fire insurance policy?"

I have heard preachers talk about the "stewardship of abundance." I have seen good and godly people dressed in fine suits. I have eaten fine food with friends. Yet, I have also heard of Christians, equally faithful, who work eighty-four-hour weeks for meager wages and barely survive.

We are looking for short-term lease apartments on Beacon Hill, one of the most expensive neighborhoods in Boston. That is where the hospital is located. I sense that it is wise to locate there. I am struggling.

A while back as I was re-reading the story of the woman at the well (John 4), I realized that she struggled, too. First she wanted an artesian well so she would never need to draw water again. What she asked in the physical realm, Jesus offered her spiritually: the refreshing and satisfying goodness and abundance of his Presence.

Is that how goodness and abundance are to be understood? Only spiritually?

The woman who anointed Jesus with costly perfume expressed great goodness and abundance in a physical way. Jesus affirmed her choice.

Can God love me through a lovely place to live in Boston? These pages are filled with stories of God's undeserved spiritual provision in my life. I am grateful. But, just as the "Why me?" question surfaces with suffering, I am also discovering that it can be raised in the midst of goodness and abundance.

► Do you struggle to receive physical blessings of goodness and abundance from God?

Open my heart and my hands, God, to know and receive whatever your love may offer.

A taste of goodness and abundance

Another of my favorite Scripture passages is Psalm 34:8: "O taste and see that the Lord is good." In my spiritual journey, I have found that concrete experiences often are the door through which I can finally perceive abstract truths about God that I struggle to comprehend.

Yesterday, I wrote about my struggles with goodness and abundance. That long-time struggle was presenting in my current life in the question about whether it would be okay with God for me to live in a lovely condo on Beacon Hill for seven weeks.

I woke this morning with an odd peace about it all. For some reason, the faces of certain members of our church and monastery community came to mind…people who have expressed deeply felt concern and sympathy for our pain and situation. People who would do anything to assist us or ease this burden. People who have seen our tears and at times cried with us. Friends who have prayed for us faithfully and given generously to the fund set up in our name.

As I thought of them, I knew, I *knew* that they would *delight* in the thought of us living in that beautiful and comfortable place. They would *rejoice* in our enjoyment of it. They would *relish* having some part in providing it for us. In their imagined faces, I saw the face of God.

Now, God's goodness and abundance aren't always defined by the provision of lovely physical things, but God certainly can use, and I daresay in this situation is using, the concrete to communicate the spiritual. Interestingly, this morning I also had an e-mail from our "African

Queen," Jenna, our daughter studying abroad in Namibia. She reported an intriguingly similar experience.

This week she is on an urban home stay with a Namibian family. For whatever reason, she was assigned to a very wealthy family. All the other students were in starkly impoverished situations while she awoke to a maid ironing her clothes. Though she'd gone to Africa to experience how the ninety percent of the world lives on ten percent of the wealth, God had a more varied experience in mind, at least for this week. Wisely, she wrote, "I'll take the experience for what it gives me." Good advice that I will take to heart as I experience a taste of goodness and abundance.

▶ Recall moments when you have tasted God's goodness and abundance on this painful journey. Have your tastes been primarily physical? Spiritual? Both?

Thank you, God, for revealing yourself in the faces and generosity of others.

❧ The everlasting arms of God

I was talking to a monk from Boston on the phone this morning. We had inquired about staying at their monastery early on in our search process. As the monk usually in charge of such inquiries, he was following up with us since he had been on vacation when our e-mail arrived. He was concerned that the brother who handled our questions had not known of any other places to which he could refer us.

I was amazed by his kindness, concern, and follow-through. Somewhere in our conversation, he mentioned a recent experience in an airplane that reminded him of the Scripture that speaks of our lives being upheld by the everlasting arms of God. As he spoke, I remembered using that same expression yesterday as I replied to an e-mail from a stranger.

A few days ago, we listed our need on Craigslist Boston, and the same day a Boston contact posted it on the Internet bulletin boards of a few large churches in the area. I have been overwhelmed by the gracious and generous e-mails.

People who have never even met us have offered support through…

Spending days with realtors looking at condos

Offering lodging

Offering advice on resources, other places to look for help

Offering furniture in case we rent an unfurnished place

Offering transportation

Contacting Boston-area friends on our behalf

Offering prayer and compassionate concern

Offering their personal stories of cancer survival

Offering to listen if we need an ear while in Boston

We are upheld, indeed embraced, by the everlasting arms of God.

► Whose arms have been the arms of God for you on this journey?

God, thank you for the body of Christ which has indeed become your everlasting arms of support and comfort to me.

✤ Déjà vu

In the midst of all the research, planning, budgeting, and anxiety, the Mystical has been inserted in two recent experiences of déjà vu.

Early this week, we saw an ad for an *ER* episode that depicted the experience of a stroke victim from the inside of her experience. Though she could not speak or communicate due to the injury, the episode let us in on her thoughts as they happened.

When Bob first saw the preview, it caught him by surprise. It was very disturbing for him because it so accurately echoed his experience of the day of the biopsy more than two months ago. He told us how frightening it was for there to be a several-second delay between watching himself rub his fingers together and actually feeling that experience he observed. Even in his stupor, he knew enough to wonder if that was permanent, and he was afraid. I shudder at the thought of his terror.

A frightening and healing déjà vu.

The second happened this morning as I woke up. One of the last things my husband and I had done last night was look at some of the digital photos our friend had taken of an apartment we are considering on Beacon Hill. It is altogether lovely, but two of my favorite features are the high ceilings and the two-story wall of paned windows on the backside of the great room.

As I was waking up this morning, I suddenly recognized the Boston living room as the room in my dream of more than a month ago. Remember the room I described in the vignette *'Big rooms are made for dancing'*? This is it! I grabbed the pictures and observed the gleaming wooden floors and the sunny yellow glow of the room.

A mystical and healing déjà vu.

▶ Have you made any somewhat mystical connections or noticed synchronicities along the way in this journey? Have any been healing?

God, in times like this, your healing embrace feels so mysteriously wonderful and so very close.

❧ Drama queen

Over the past week, I've become aware that I have a real fear of being seen as a drama queen. These questions have risen in my heart:

What if everything turns out absolutely fine?

What if these treatments are a piece of cake and we have a great time in Boston and our son goes back to law school and on with his life as if nothing ever happened?

Certainly, that is my fondest hope. But will people think I exaggerated the seriousness of all this?

Have I exaggerated the seriousness of all this?

Have I overreacted?

Have I been a drama queen?

Now, there's the real concern.

In these pages, I have poured out much of my internal experience of these events. I feel deeply and have expressed that depth. Is that fanciful drama or deep authenticity?

Perhaps the question is: "Have I been describing or performing? Offering vulnerably or manipulating?"

Or, is the question: "Do only certain levels of tragedy warrant certain levels of emotional response? Do I really need a tragic ending to validate my painful emotional experiences along the way?"

Or even: "What's wrong with drama queens? What baggage do I attach to the open expression of intense emotion?"

Or: "Am I simply feeling vulnerable in my openness and looking for a way to invalidate myself before others do it for me?"

Am I a drama queen?

▶ What kinds of feelings or questions have arisen for you in the wake of expressing deep emotions during this painful journey?

God, I have such a hard time owning and expressing my emotions. Why is it that I always seem to want to shame myself for feeling?

✣ To receive

I've never been very good at receiving. I don't quite know why. Whether the issue was words of comfort, constructive criticism, or even a compliment, there's something within my soul that resists letting the words of others penetrate my heart.

Giving is easier; less frightening and more comfortable for me.

I noticed today, though, that that is changing, primarily because of my new faith community. When we first came to this church, I was in a very painful season in my life. We had spent the previous year in Seattle where I had gone to graduate school, a wonderfully enriching experience. When it was time to leave, the rest of my family outvoted me and we returned to Texas. To say that I was sad would be a gross understatement.

Ready for a change, we chose a new church tradition, attending a liturgical church for the first time. About the same time, we became acquainted with two Benedictine monks at a local monastery. From the very beginning the quiet beauty and gentle rhythm of the liturgy became a healing sanctuary for my soul. There were many, many days when I would worship with tears flowing in a steady stream.

The people of our new community were compassionate and deeply respectful of me, offering comfort without questions, safety and presence without prying. It is as if they had such an understanding of the healing Presence of God in this place that they were just glad I was there. For whatever reason, the "brand" of comfort they offered was a match for my soul and I began to learn to receive.

As healing happened, I became an integral and contributing part of our lively, growing community, quickly reverting to my more comfortable role as a giver.

But in these months of tumor journey, once again there has been a shift. At a goodbye brunch for our pastor yesterday, so very many people asked about our son. I was amazed. I received their compassion and care, often offered through sincere and moist eyes, or strong and tender hugs. And I recognized within myself that this willingness and ability to receive their comfort was something new in my life, something that these gracious people have taught me. This community has taught my soul how to receive.

▶ How comfortable are you in the role of the receiver? To what degree has that been a challenge as you have walked this path of pain?

God, some days I am so grateful to you and those around me that I actually ache. How can I ever, ever say "thank you" enough?

❧ Blessed to be a blessing

This morning in church we heard again the story of Abraham's calling from Genesis 12. What struck me was the fact that God said he was blessing Abraham so that he could be a blessing to others.

Blessed to be a blessing. I immediately thought of the myriad of ways God has blessed us through our family and faith community. In only a few short days, enough money has been raised to cover our housing expenses and our flights to and from Boston. And we are talking about a lovely one-bedroom condo just a five-minute walk from the hospital.

Blessed to be a blessing. I think perhaps the social scientist Abraham Maslow had some wisdom in his hierarchy of needs. The premise is that once our basic needs are met, then and only then can we begin to engage thoughts of caring for others. Now, I wish I could say that I had such amazing confidence in God's promises that I could transcend such basic patterns, but alas, if I am honest, the relief I feel in this moment exposes the fact that I have in no way leapt over my own needs.

Only now can I begin to wonder who I might meet while I am in Boston. Whom might my blessed life bless? Perhaps it will be my son. Maybe I will be able to make this lovely place feel like home for him, offering some comfort in a scary time. Maybe my peaceful spirit will bless him. Perhaps it will just be the readers of my book. Perhaps I have been blessed in order to edit well and bless my readers that way. Perhaps it will be someone we meet at the hospital, staff or fellow patients. Only God knows God's intent.

Blessed to be a blessing. What I do know is that I now see the blessing I have received as a stewardship, a throughway, not an end point. Through me, the love of my community will be multiplied in the kingdom at large. It is the way God has worked for many, many, many years. As a daughter of Abraham, I have been blessed to be a blessing.

▶ Have you received any blessings along the way that have allowed you to then bless others?

God, thank you for meeting my needs. Open my eyes to the needs of others.

❧ In the flow

One of my favorite things about traveling by air is that I get such an awesome "big picture" view of creation below. This revelation of God has taught me so much through the years, and this flight to California was no different.

Among my favorite things to observe are landforms and rivers. I will never cease to be amazed by God's creative side and God's apparent disregard for efficiency. When men want to get from point "A" to point "B," they build a highway, straight as they possibly can. When God wants to get from point "A" to point "B," God shapes a gently winding river. Not nearly as "efficient" but far more fun!

As I enjoyed the twisty rivers below, my own story came to mind. Though it is tempting to call this tumor journey a "detour" or a distraction, or an interruption in my newly found journey toward calling, the wisdom of the river tells me it is not. It is in the flow.

For some reason, it is necessary to cover this ground in this way. What is it in me that prefers to section, parcel, analyze, and systematize my life rather than simply live in the wonder of its flow?

Will I trust the One who shapes this river of my life?

Will I let go of my need to see and know how it all fits together?

Will I miss this moment in an effort to control or prepare for the next one?

Will I dare to let the water splash in my face?

Will I engage the rapids with laughter or fear?

Will I resist or learn to live well in the flow?

▶ Do you picture your current suffering in the flow of your life and journey or as a detour or interruption?

God, I am so drawn to the wisdom and freedom of the river. I want to live this way so, so bad; yet, I feel so far from it.

Subtly answered prayer

I love synchronicities, those magical moments when the ordinary things in life line up in such a way that I see the work of God in the arrangement. The other day, as I was flying home from California, I experienced such a moment.

As I have written previously, it was a difficult decision to make this trip. I had offered to do a workshop for a new organization, PASCH (Peace and Safety in the Christian Home), long before this tumor journey commenced. Though confident that the material in my book would be healing for women in that horrible life circumstance, I was tempted to back out. I also had many fears about venturing into the "big room" of the larger national scene.

When all of our medically related obligations lined up around these dates, I faced my fears, made the choice to go, and gave my workshop on the first afternoon. The conference was housed in a newly remodeled sanctuary with a stunning glass ceiling. My eyes were continually drawn to the ceiling and bright blue sky above. My soul drank in the open space as I learned and worshiped, and enjoyed the folks at the conference.

On the flight home, the plane flew just above a floor of clouds almost the entire four-hour trip. Again, the sky was blue, and this lovely expanse of wide-open space fed my soul. Again, I could not seem to stop gazing out the window, pondering the expanse.

Then I remembered my prayer of more than two years ago. Though I do not recall the specific set of circumstances that first prompted this deeply felt and long held prayer, I remember the longing for open spaces with clarity. In fact, my husband gifted me with a lovely sky-blue-and-white watercolor meditation with this verse scripted at the bottom: He brought me out into a broad place; he delivered me, because he delighted in me (Psalm 18:19).

For two years, those words have hung just next to my computer. For two years, God has been at work creating open spaces: large windows from Boston to California, opportunities to engage women from all over the world. I feel the delight of God as I connect the broad blue sky to the blue and white picture to the promises of God. I am thankful that I let my eyes be drawn to these spaces and that I did not altogether miss this subtly answered prayer.

▶ Think back to prayers of your own. Has God answered in small or large ways?

I love you, God, because you have heard my voice.

🌿 Transitions

It feels as if my life is currently in a transitional middle space in many arenas.

I am beginning to prepare to live in Boston for seven weeks. It is four weeks until we leave. I am not quite here and not quite there. Even once I am there, I will be almost here again.

I am waiting for my editor to contact me and begin the foreign process of editing my first book. The manuscript is complete, yet not complete.

We are waiting for the paperwork to be completed for the lease in Boston. It is negotiated but not finalized.

The investigative phase of this tumor journey is transitioning to the treatment phase.

I am transitioning from a chaplain to a published writer. I may transition to a doctoral student.

I am transitioning from a nearly full-time mom to an empty nester, from the mother of dependent children to the mom of adult children.

This litany reminds me of the moment in the airplane last week when we were descending through the clouds as we landed. I could see the land but could not make out any specific forms or see enough to locate myself on a map. It was a mystical moment, full of hope and faith, anticipation and longing.

I have an intuitive sense that my life is at a breakpoint. The place I find myself when I land will be like no other place I have known, internally and externally. It is a frightening and exciting thought.

In the midst of straining to see what is to come, I do not want to miss the wonder of this middle point. The fresh beauty and mystery of those few seconds in the descending plane let me know that I have missed far too many of these kinds of moments in my life. So doggedly fixed on securing the future, I often miss the present. I miss the magic of transitions.

▶ What transitions or middle spaces are you negotiating on your journey?

Oh God, give me eyes to see and the courage to experience the unique gifts found only in these fleeting middle moments.

❧ Everywhere I turn

Everywhere I turn this morning, the world seems bent on inciting me to anger:

The Realtor's fee on the condo in Boston is twice what we expected.

Gary, the healing pug, needs to go out and simply wants to wander.

My garden shouts its need for spring attention: transplanting, pruning, and weed pulling.

We got a collections notice in the mail on a bill the insurance company said they paid. Why didn't the provider call us before they turned it over to collections?

I get a recorded message when I call to try to correct the problem.

My walking shoes have developed a deep crack in one of the soles and need to be replaced.

My exercise pants don't have pockets to hold the cell phone, so I need to wait on a call back before I can walk.

I feel weak with anger.

Finally, I go for a walk on this beautiful spring day with my cell phone precariously tucked in a jacket pocket tied around my waist.

The sky is brilliant blue. The flashy pink azaleas are beginning to bloom. Fresh budding leaves give the oaks a golden glow. Down the street a neighbor has planted crocus bulbs that are blooming beautifully, bluish purple, a rare sight in our climate. I spot some daffodils that have sprung up in the middle of a lawn, announcing our early Texas spring with their yellow trumpets.

Though I write about what I see, somehow today the beauty won't sink in. I see it and want to be inspired and comforted by it, but I am not. Perhaps the problem is not rooted in what I encounter, frustrating or lovely. What is it that has my heart locked up so tight that all I feel is anger everywhere I turn?

▶ Along the way, have you been caught or stuck in one emotion or another?

God, I am stuck. I could use some help here; but, sadly, I'm not sure even you can get through to my heart today. Help. Please, help.

✢ Creating a new past

What is it about approaching forty that wakes our souls from a previously oblivious state? I know of a career counseling company that refuses to accept clients under that age. They believe that in the first half of our lives we operate more on energy than wisdom or giftedness. Though Bob disagrees with me, I think they have a good point.

I made that forty-something transition a number of years ago. My wake-up call actually came at age thirty-five. I suddenly realized that I had lived most of my life more like a "ministry machine" than a woman in relationship with God and others. I learned quite young to cover all human need, beauty, desire, and emotion with a heavy blanket of competence, production, and performance. Any pain or loss I encountered during that past reality of personhood was quickly intellectualized, dismissed, or simply denied. I did not "do" winters of the soul. I did not know what grief even felt like. Sadly, that worked well for far too long.

I realized the other day that one of the gifts of this tumor journey is that I am creating a new past for myself. Now, before I continue, it is important to note that I consider even my healthier choices, though mine, to be completely rooted in grace, undeserved favors from God. So, perhaps better said, with God's help, I have made significantly different choices that have resulted in a significantly different experience. The new present I am now living will soon become my new past.

For instance, I have not only allowed time for my grief, I have chosen to actively engage it. Consequently, I am living with more freedom, less "baggage," more ability to focus on other things like living out my calling. In honoring my humanness with its inherent needs and limitations, I am becoming more human, more present, more available to myself, others, and God. I am amazed at the difference. I have also chosen to share my intimate, personal experience of this journey with a few others along the way. Now, mind you, these friends are carefully chosen, safe people. Nevertheless, this, too, is different for me. I feel the greater vulnerability to my core but have chosen it anyway.

This choice also is birthing a different experience for me. Because people around me know my pain, they can offer me comfort, concrete comfort evidenced as hugs, prayers, cards, fundraising efforts and gifts of money. I feel their comfort; I am relieved of significant and large parts of this burden. As Isaiah says, I find myself trading ashes for a beautiful garland, tears for joy, and weariness for praise. Together, God, the community, and I are creating a new past.

▶ In what way does your journey thus far reflect new choices and fresh patterns in your life, a new past in the making?

God, only you would "give them a garland instead of ashes, the oil of gladness instead of mourning, the mantle of praise instead of a faint spirit." Isaiah 61:3

❧ You can't have him

My husband's Aunt Jane died this week after a long illness. Yesterday, we went to her funeral. It was lovely and a wonderful reflection on a life well lived.

Since my husband was a pallbearer and we were driving from out of town the morning of the funeral, we allowed plenty of time for traffic and weather. Encountering rain but no traffic, we arrived well ahead of others.

As my husband, Robert, was busy receiving instructions and his boutonniere, I said my private goodbyes to Jane. She was the aunt with the ever-welcoming face who restored a huge Georgian mansion in Navasota, Texas, with her own hands. She was the genealogist of the family and an avid gardener. Always curious, always learning, always laughing, always in motion. In her "old age," she took on a new venture of planting a vineyard on a plot of land on her husband's cotton farm. Her first crop was so amazing she even made the front page of the *Houston Post*. Though I am grieved by her death, I can celebrate that Jane lived a full, passionate, and long life.

In the midst of pleasant memories, I felt an unexpected and fierce surge of rage toward God. "You cannot have him. You can't have my son yet." I was instantly back in the Intensive Care Unit of M.D. Anderson Hospital, waiting for Bob to wake up. At the same time, I projected our story forward and could see myself in Boston, living out my fears of encountering another round of unexpected and unexplainable side effects of treatment.

I may have been this angry with God before, but I've never dared to feel it or own it in the way I did yesterday. I understood Jacob's fight with the angel like never before. If push comes to shove, it will indeed be a battle.

My internal distance from surrender to God on this matter frightens me; yet I know, at least for now, there is no sense of backing down.

I say again to God, in a prayer of sorts, a new kind of prayer for me, "You can't have him."

▶ Have you encountered any moments of unexpected rage? Toward God or others?

Though I am admittedly shaking with fear as I pray, you can't have him, God. God, please, please, don't take him from me.

✿ I am home

The thought of leaving home for seven weeks is a bit unsettling for me. Though I love to travel, this feels very different than going somewhere for the sake of exploration and adventure.

I suppose it is all in the perspective. I could see this as only an extended adventure but somehow that doesn't feel quite honest. Though we certainly plan to have a good time, we are there for medical treatment. Bob has a brain tumor. He may not feel well. He may want a sense of home for the simple comfort of it all. I may, too.

As I have begun to name these anxieties, comfort has come in the form of a reminder of an unusual insight I had a few years ago. I was doing a retreat for a women's group and, as I often do, I had planned the time to include teaching as well as self-reflective exercises and quiet time.

We opened the time by introducing ourselves using art cards—postcards of famous works of art—selected by each woman from 300-plus options. I encouraged the women to keep their chosen card with them throughout the weekend and see if they saw even more in their selection than they had initially. My card was a picture of a sculpture of a nude woman, kneeling on a rock and stretching toward the sky. I had also asked the women to select a slip of paper from a jar full of sixty or so other reflection exercises.

As I sometimes do, I found a few moments of quiet and did a few of the exercises myself. I took my card out and put it beside my journal as I opened my slip of paper. Mine said, "Sketch you internal image of home."

Suddenly, the two connected: *I* am home. Home does not reside outside of me, it *is* me. I have all I need for life, safety, and goodness within. Christ dwells in me.

And because *I* am home, I *am* home and I am *home*. I don't need to put so much energy into lining up all the externals to be just so. I can rest and dwell securely in the simplicity and sufficiency of my own personhood.

As I anticipate moving to Boston, I am comforted by the reminder that I am home.

▶ How has your own journey of pain influenced your sense or definition of "home"?

Christ, in you I live and move and have my being. I am home.

❧ The brain and big things

I have often said to families in the hospital: "A little information can bring a lot of comfort." I'm finding that true for myself these days. I learned something new about the brain yesterday. It seems that the part of the brain that stores a record of our experiences is not the same part that creates understanding of those experiences. A large part of incorporating new life experiences involves moving information from the sensing part to the processing part. In a way, we metabolize experiences as we metabolize food.

In everyday life, that process moves along pretty well. However, when big things, traumatic things, come into our realm of experience, the process becomes problematic. You see, the passageway between the two parts of the brain is a bit like a straw. Trying to process trauma is like attempting to channel water from a fire hose through a straw.

As I have said before, I am deeply thankful for the gentle pace of this journey. It has allowed me to process experiences as they are encountered. Thus far, my experiment has "worked." Now, I know why it has worked.

As I have also said before, I sometimes fear being overwhelmed by life. This understanding of biology helps me not only understand the pain of being overwhelmed as a biological phenomenon but also gives me confidence in my ability to process even very traumatic experiences given time and opportunity.

Ah, but I sense there is more to this than what mere knowledge of biology and time can address. I remember my deeply and intensely angry heart at Aunt Jane's funeral yesterday. That fierce determination within me felt as if it came from some place that I am not sure any amount of processing could reach.

Perhaps that's the place where grace and grace alone becomes the healer.

So, I will pray for grace to deal with the parts of my heart I simply cannot access. I will be faithful to process what I can as I celebrate my newfound knowledge regarding the brain and big things.

▶ How is your current approach to processing your painful journey working? Are there parts of your heart not yet being addressed?

God, you have searched me and known me. Heal me, God, heal all of me. But, lest you forget, first heal my son.

A new translation

Life experiences often translate unseeable spiritual truths into terms I can better understand, remember, and absorb. For example, I previously wrote about how my experiences in giving birth to our children have informed larger life lessons regarding enduring pain.

This current experience of friends and family paying our way to live in Boston is another translation experience for me. Through it, I am coming to know the gospel, the good news about Jesus, in a more profound way. I sense that God is inviting me, even daring me, to really embrace a new kind of provision.

I am a saver. I hoard experiences, emotions, money, time, wisdom, affirmation, thanksgiving, and my abilities. Yet, in this moment, I sense that God wants me to spend. Even more disturbingly, to spend what *others* have earned. Though it may sound ridiculous to many of you, that is quite a difficult challenge for me. In fact, it is a faith venture.

I am beginning to recognize that perhaps there is a shadow side to my penchant to save. To the extent that I can save in life, I do not need God. I use saving to establish my independence and control over a life that feels out of my control. I know it's an illusion: I am dependent upon God for my very breath. But it is a very deeply ingrained illusion nonetheless. I also use saving as a way I seek to earn God's approval by proving my thriftiness. Ugh. So, spending is a faith venture for me.

I got a similar taste of this translated gospel a few years ago when I prepared a fabulous dessert for friends. On the one hand, my friends were hesitant to consume the layered chocolate mousse parfait over which I had slaved for days. *Hours* in the making. Minutes on the tongue. Forever on the hips! On the other hand, that is what it was made for. To *not* consume it would be the tragedy. Once consumed, the dessert became not only a good memory but also a "taste" of God's grace, a sensual experience of the ample abundance of God's generous love.

Through the specific intent and generosity of others, we have enough money to not only live on Beacon Hill in a nice condo five minutes from the hospital, but to eat out some, go to a ball game or two, take in a museum and a concert, and travel a bit on weekends. I not only do not have to worry about money, I can enjoy myself at others' expense. My only task is to be grateful and enjoy the gift. The gospel, the good news of Jesus, is alive for me in a new translation.

▶ In what ways are you living God's good news and generosity? Laughter? Provision? Healing? Comfort? Support?

God, your goodness and generosity invite me to hope for more, to hope and pray, once more, for healing.

❧ The squeaky wheel

You know what they say about the squeaky wheel…it usually gets the grease. Often, that is a true saying. But perhaps there is more to that expression than a simple observation.

I realized the other day that that expression is almost always used as a criticism of the squeaky wheel. A squeak is not a very pleasant sound, rather offensive and bothersome. It seems to imply that it is unfair or less noble for the wheel to squeak, to need and ask for grease so it can run more efficiently, as if by squeaking it is demanding too much attention, stealing grease from other needy wheels.

I wonder if our use of that phrase doesn't belie our American penchant for individualism, a penchant we sometimes value even to the point of our own demise. Perhaps it is a way to subtly shame the inherent (and appropriate!) neediness within us all.

Let's face it: We were not designed to be able to make it in this world apart from the help of some sort of community. And for many of us, that is a frightening thought. Who among us has not, at some point, been let down if not outright betrayed by those on whom we were relying? This help we need is not always reliably available. It seems far safer to pretend we can make it on our own.

The squeaky wheel gets the grease. You might guess that I feel a bit like a squeaky wheel getting some grease right now. Having been willing to express my pain, anxiety, and financial need and receiving amazingly generous help, I am struggling a bit with my new "greased" status.

It is inviting me to own the reality of my dependence on others in new ways, a fact much more easily embraced in the abstract than in the concrete. On some level, I am thankful that I have dared to be the squeaky wheel. The grease feels good. And, even more so, the willingness to vulnerably connect feels like God's intent for God's people.

But, I'm struggling to offload the shame I associate with my neediness. No matter how much my mind tries to justify the appropriateness of my humanness with its inherent limitations, I still wince as I think of myself as the squeaky wheel.

▶ Have you been a squeaky wheel or are you more apt to suffer in independent silence? How do you feel about your choice?

God, I find living more honestly in community to be both wonderful and terrifying. Wonder-laced terror: I guess that's pretty much the norm for those who followed you.

✤ Undoing my bind

As I have said before, I am a performer. I learned early in life that the way to obtain inclusion and approval was to perform well, to be competent and productive in my world. I used that approach in school, at home, and at church. And it worked well for many years. I was a successful performer, earning inclusion and approval on a regular basis, from parents, teachers, and friends. But there is also a dark side to that role.

Successful performers have a very hard time experiencing grace. We have a natural affinity for justice, making sure we are always on the "winning" side. We connect all the good in our lives to what we have done, fostering the illusion of having earned the good. And, I readily admit that it is only an illusion: Grace is all around me, supporting me every day. It's just that the driven performer in me doesn't allow me to *feel* what I *know* to be true.

Those of us performers who happen to be Christians are in an additional bind. Theologically, we believe that our lives depend on grace, that we rely on Jesus' sacrifice instead of our own merits. We are grateful for the grace that saves our souls. Theologically.

But, most often, the illusion of earning my way is too strong. The determined self-sufficiency is too deeply ingrained. It is a tough bind to break. Yet one that I sense is breaking down just a bit in my life right now.

I know that I know that I do not "carry my weight" in my faith community. And, amazingly, they love me anyway! Amazingly, they ask me about my son with tears in their eyes. Amazingly they give money so we can know comfort in Boston. There is no judgment, no evaluation of worthiness. I have not earned such love or inclusion or approval through performance. I have not done a thing for them. Yet, they love me. Through their love, affection, and generosity, God is allowing me to experience a level of grace I have not been conscious of before. God is releasing me from this self-imposed prison of performance. God is undoing my bind.

▶ When have you tasted grace along the way in your journey? How is that changing your experience of God?

God, grace and peace are sourced in you and experienced in the faces who surround me. I stand amazed.

Aching gratitude

Have you ever been so grateful that it actually hurt? The first time that happened in my life was many years ago on a Friday night, just after a vacation Bible school closing program.

At the time, we were attending a small Bible church in our area. As in previous years, we had chosen to write our own curriculum and were heavily invested both in the program and the people. For the first time that year, we had invited children from a local day care center to take part in our week of learning and fun.

The results were astonishing. Our team worked together beautifully all week. Each day we saw God's Spirit at work weaving each person's unique giftedness into the jobs at hand. Skits, snacks, teaching time, crafts, music, recreation; it all flowed with a single message of the love of Christ. The whole was definitely greater than the sum of the parts could ever have been. The children seemed to soak up the affection and new knowledge. We were so thankful to offer both.

Our closing program that Friday night was a real crescendo moment. The room filled with laughter and tears as we watched slides of the week. The good news of the gospel was in the air and expressed in so many ways that night. You could see the love of Christ on the faces of the children.

As the director of the VBS that week, perhaps I saw more because of my freedom to float throughout the week. My heart was full to the point of bursting. As we were cleaning up after the program that night, it occurred to me that I was so thankful I was actually in pain. My body ached to express gratitude for all that I had experienced. Words did not seem enough. Even prayer felt inadequate. I knew of no way to release it all— so I ached with gratitude.

In recent days, I have sensed again that familiar ache. Oddly, I noticed for a while that that pain was even keeping me from doing what I could to express my thanks, like writing notes to those who had given. Because of the inadequacy of my grateful response, my tendency was to not engage it at all.

After such wrestling, I have concluded that aching gratitude is a bit like arthritis: You can either let it paralyze you or discover that the ache subsides as you do what you can to exercise and act on aching gratitude.

▶ Describe moments of gratitude in your journey. How have you responded to them?

"For you are great and do wondrous things; you alone are God." Psalm 86:10

❧ Giving up for Lent

Having become a part of a liturgical tradition in recent years, I have been intrigued by how often God initiates things in my life through the seasons of the church calendar. Advent, Christmas, Epiphany, Ordinary time, Lent, Easter, and Pentecost. On more than one occasion, I have seen God working in my life in rhythm with the energy of each season.

For example, Lent is a time of giving up things for the sake of listening more attentively to God. There are some things I have initiated to give up for Lent, and some things God seems to have initiated on my behalf:

By my intention—

Overeating. No second helpings.

Sugar. No desserts.

Physical stress. Add bi-weekly massages. Sometimes letting go can be quite enjoyable.

By God's invitation—

Independent spiritedness as I fulfill my vow to share my experience of this tumor journey.

Self-sufficiency as I receive the financial help of others.

The safety of a small room as I go to California to bring my vision to an international audience.

Thriftiness as we sign a lease for a lovely and expensive condo on Beacon Hill.

Suffering alone as I let the tears of others soothe my soul.

My prison of performance-based approval and inclusion as I experience a rare and wonderful taste of pure grace.

What amazing invitations from God. Indeed, I am hearing the voice of God in new ways, with new clarity. What life-changing things to be giving up for Lent.

▶ Make a list of small or large things you are giving up, by intention or by invitation.

O God, may these offerings open my heart to you in new ways.

❧ Drowning in details

I feel as if I am drowning in details:

Determining flight dates and times for my husband and daughter to join us means juggling

Two personal calendars; a busy career and a high school senior's spring semester

Blackout dates, if we want to use donated tickets

Direct versus indirect flights; our daughter is hesitant about changing planes

Arrival times; we don't want to be out too late in case Bob is tired from the treatments

Departure times; they don't want to leave too early because they have a two-hour pre-flight drive to Houston

Making provision to work on my book means

Finding a computer to use

Finding a way to access e-mail while there

Locating a printer to pack or buying one there

Finding a way to bring all my hard-copy files with me

Maximizing insurance means

Forms, forms, forms—referrals, proof of insurance, medical records

Interpreting insurance explanation of benefits

Appealing inaccuracies

Keeping a record of whom we saw when

Tracking who files what when

Sorting bills versus statements from providers

Evaluating deductibles and maximum out-of-pockets

Paying what we owe

Getting insurance to pay in a timely manner so we don't get turned over to collection agencies!

The lease involves

Credit reports

Lead law forms

Application forms

Though I am I writer, I do not deal well with paper. I am not a detail person. I am currently drowning in details.

- What new skills have you acquired on this journey? What limitations has it exposed?

God, help! Give me patience with the details, but even more so, give me patience with my own limitations.

❧ Elusive acceptance

For most of my adult life, I have had "issues" with my feet. At thirty-one, I had surgery for bilateral Morton's neuromas, bundles of nerves that formed on the ball of the foot. Within the same year, I discovered that the source of seven years of chronic back pain was a difference in the length of my legs. The solution: a three-quarter-inch lift attached to the bottom of my shoe. I soon discovered that not every shoe could be fitted with a lift. I gave away many shoes.

Then, more than three years ago I was also diagnosed with plantar fasciitis, an inflammation of the fascia near the heel of my left foot. I was told it would be slow to heal and that I would need custom-made insoles for the rest of my life to prevent recurrence. I heard the "slow to heal" part but not the "rest of your life" part.

The reason I know I didn't hear that part is because, more than three years later, I am throwing away all my shoes that cannot be fitted with an insole. As with the lift, not all could accommodate that adaptation. I found it odd that I had hung on to them for such a long time. Believe me, it is *not* because we have abundant closet space in our sixty-year-old home!

I concluded that true acceptance is pretty elusive. Even this relatively small loss took me more than three years to really absorb. Where am I with regard to Bob's tumor?

A part of me wants to refuse to even address that question because it all feels way too undetermined at this point. I don't yet know the full extent of that adjustment; hopefully, it will be very small.

But another part of me knows that reasoning is simply an attempt to dodge the question. No matter how this is resolved, it is an ordeal in the moment. It is an important and traumatic part of our collective story. Our family medical history has changed forever. There is cancer in our gene pool.

Though I do not know how close to acceptance I am, this I do know: I still tear up pretty quickly when I speak about Bob's tumor with others.

I still have many, many, many processing thoughts to be recorded in this collection of vignettes, each one moving me closer to that ever-elusive acceptance.

▶ To what degree have you accepted your painful journey? Can you put a percentage number to your degree of acceptance?

God, even as I pray for acceptance, I can feel that angry part of me rising within in protest of the whole ordeal. Perhaps I need to pray harder.

✻ Inhumane expectations

I used to call them "superhuman" expectations but now I've decided that "inhumane" is a more appropriate choice of words.

I still want to believe I can get away with being superhuman but I don't want anything to do with being inhumane.

For the past week I have battled my internal expectations without much success. It came to a head on Monday. That morning I called the dentist to see about getting an appointment to deal with a tooth that had been increasingly bothersome. I just wanted it looked at sometime before we were to leave for Boston three weeks or so from now. His receptionist said they had just had a cancellation so I could come right in.

Though I had neither walked nor showered, I threw on some clothes and went. Hours later, I got out just in time to make Noon Prayer at the monastery. Then I rushed home, ate a quick lunch, showered, and was off to meet with spiritual direction clients for the remainder of my afternoon, barely fitting in the task of picking up some insurance forms from my husband and getting the packet in the mail as I had promised.

As I was driving home after my last appointment, the internal assault of my thoughts was ruthless. I knew the shape of the house to which I was returning: sink and counter full of unwashed dishes, dirty clothes, a desk piled with bills, an unmade bed, and this and that here and there everywhere! No groceries were bought for the refrigerator; no plans for dinner had been made. What kind of a woman was I anyway?

That did it. That internal voice had gone just a little too far and the wise woman in me began to fight back. I had been neither foolish nor lazy with my time. I finally saw that litany of superhuman expectations for just what it was: the inhumane treatment of my very own soul.

There are only so many hours in a day. It is human to have limitations; humane and dignified, not shameful. There is no such thing as "superhuman." Even Jesus who was fully God and fully human was not superhuman. That expression is a misnomer that attempts to put a positive, attractive spin on a kind of bondage to which many in our culture have surrendered. I for one will continue to fight to respect the dignity of my human limitations. I am renaming those rambling demands that float about in my head on days like last Monday. From now on, they will be inhumane expectations.

▶ Do you have superhuman/inhumane expectations of yourself even in the midst of a season of pain?

God, you respond to my human frailty and limitation with compassion. Teach me to do the same.

Eastering

I know that Easter is usually used as a noun. But, in the spiritual realm, I think it is a verb. At least that's how I experience it every year—as the process of new growth, the unfolding of a new layer of change in my life.

About this time into the season of Lent, four or five weeks, I begin to get a sense of the new work God is doing in my soul. It usually reveals itself in small clues. I have four thus far.

The first came last week when I took a different seat at Morning Prayer. From this spot in the room, I could see more blue sky beyond the trees than I usually can. I experienced a new view. I wondered: Is this new work of God in my life actually, really, permanently changing my vision? Will I come out of this with a lasting reshaping of my perspective?

The second clue came a few days later when I put words to how disorienting this experience of receiving grace has been in my spiritual life. As I have said before, as one given to "doing," I have a natural bent toward justice, toward earning my way, living within my means. This experience of living off the generosity of others is new for me and quite disconcerting. I wonder—will I dare to really embrace a life of grace? Will I let my soul expand or remain safe in my familiar but limited patterns of living?

The third clue. After packing to go out of town with my husband this week, I had a window of time, about forty-five minutes, before he would arrive to pick me up. As I looked at the unfolded laundry, the unswept floor, the uncleared desk, I said a quick prayer, "Oh, Lord, what would you have me do?" From somewhere inside me, the ancient question from the Garden of Eden rose, "Where are you?" I sensed God's invitation to stop for these few minutes and locate myself. As I picked up my watercolors, I replied, "This is just like you, God." I wonder…is my understanding of God changing? Am I really beginning to believe that

God wants my heart and my presence more than my faithfulness and dutiful service?

The final clue might seem like the strangest to many of you. It is the color yellow. Now, I do not believe that I am literally encountering this color more in my life these days, but I am certain that I am noticing it more often. To me, it is the color of joy, the color of new life, the color of glory, the color of spring, the color of warmth, the color of Eastering.

▶ What new life is this challenging journey birthing in you? Perhaps some new understanding of God, yourself, or others? Or new ways of living or responding?

O God, complete this new work you have begun in my soul.

❧ Alarmed

Here I am again. Alarmed at my son's behavior.

He came home from work today and told me the fire alarm had gone off in their building this afternoon. He works at a law office housed in a high-rise downtown.

He said that he didn't leave.

He checked e-mail instead and sent off some replies.

He even smelled smoke. Or he thought it might have been smoke. He wasn't sure.

He said everyone else left.

He said he'd had too many false alarms and fire drills in high school to react.

He said he calculated his risk and he felt fine about his decision.

I am alarmed.

Am I overreacting?

Was he the smart one?

Was he utterly foolish?

Is this the "mild euphoria" that can come when your hypothalamus doesn't get enough oxygen?

He is not alarmed by alarms.

I, however, am alarmed.

▶ In this season of struggle, whose behavior has been the most troublesome to you?

Okay, God, I really need some help here. I am alarmed and yet, I also have no idea what love looks like in this moment.

✤ This interruption in normal

Our son leaves today for his spring break trip with his old college buds. Four young men will pile into a small Saturn and drive twenty-five plus hours, nonstop, from Texas to Connecticut to see a fifth friend now at Yale Divinity School. I contributed a six-pound jar of peanut butter.

Bob has been planning this trip for months. It has definitely been a bright spot in a socially dull spring. He can't wait to go.

I have felt the tension building all week. Between Bob and me, between Bob and Beaumont, between Bob and work hours, between Bob and undone laundry, between Bob and anything that might keep him from leaving as soon as possible for someplace other than here.

The night before the day he is to leave, I mention that he might want to do some laundry. He goes out with a friend who's home on break from a different school.

The next morning he is angry because the washer isn't immediately available. He is late for work. He comes home early so he can leave as soon as possible. He doesn't even work the thirty hours he is allowed as a part-time employee.

I am angry. I feel like he has violated an agreement. I let him know.

He feels controlled, like he's being treated as a child. He complains about unclear expectations.

And he's right. We haven't been clear. We don't know how to treat him right now—like a normal adult or like a sick child or something in between.

He is our firstborn. This transition would be a challenge under the best of circumstances.

I sense that we are missing some important stage of normal relational growth. The negotiation of this transition of parent/child to adult/adult child is all screwed up. We are both upset. We are both suffering. !@#$%! this interruption in normal!

▶ What normal relational transitions have been disrupted along your path?

It is lost, God. Any hope of normal seems hopelessly lost. I feel lost, too, and sad. Somehow, God, please preserve our relationship in the midst of this mess.

❧ Living in layers

In recent days, I have often sensed that I am living my life with many layers of personal experience, all woven together as they are lived, yet in moments, able to be seen distinctly.

For instance, when someone makes a simple inquiry like, "How's it going?" I generally and sincerely reply, "Fine." The layer of my life that is closest to the surface seems, in most moments, relatively unruffled by our tumor journey. Thankfully, and uniquely, this has been a bit of a slow-motion trauma, unfolding with a gentleness that has left the surface of any single day relatively undisturbed. That layer really is fine.

I got an e-mail the other day from a good friend who inquired, "So how's your heart doing?" Though I was not surprised to get that question from that caring friend, I was surprised by my response. I couldn't really answer his question. On that day when I would have easily said I was "fine" to a surface inquiry, I did not really know the state of my heart. Furthermore, and probably more importantly, I did not even want to try to figure it out. "What's up with that?" I wondered. My guess is that that layer wasn't doing so well.

A few days later, I woke up realizing that I had spent a large part of the previous night running through the plethora of my concerns about our son's anticipated radiation treatments. Throughout the night, I had rehearsed the risks over and over again at that level of consciousness between wakefulness and sleep. There is a layer of my life that continues to harbor significant anxiety about all this.

I think perhaps there are many, many more layers—like the one that surfaced at Aunt Jane's funeral when something in me suddenly raged at God, "You can't have him!" And the layers full of bits of wisdom and new growth. And yet another huge layer overflowing with gratitude.

I do not know if living in trying times such as these makes such layered living more of a reality or simply more easily seen. Whatever the case, it is my reality for now: living in layers.

▶ Can you describe your current reality in terms of layered living?

Thank you, God, for loving all of me, every layer, at every moment, lovely or not. How I need your love.

Missing seasons

A little over a month ago, I realized that I completely missed this past season of winter. I walked out the door one day and the air smelled like spring, that fresh, damp, almost musty smell of new growth. I looked up and my oak tree was not golden with the pollen of the first blush of new growth, it was green with small leaves.

"It can't be spring! Where did the winter go?" I had virtually no memories of being outside in the crisp air, of watching the weather on TV in anticipation of the next cold front, of taking in the barrenness of the season. At least not enough memories to make up three months' worth of winter. Yet as I looked around, it was indeed spring. Distracted by our tumor journey, I missed last winter.

Today was supposed to be a day given to writing. I am "behind" on my recording practice and looked forward to a day of catching up. Today, however, was also the day that Gary, our "spring breaking" son's pup, decided to eat a small package of chocolate he found on the floor, foil and all. After consulting on the phone with my husband, I administered a dose of salt to induce vomiting and sat with Gary outside waiting…and waiting…and waiting.

As we waited, I looked around at my garden. I noticed the loropetalum that has almost taken over one corner of our house. I saw the yellow Brazilian plume that is now as tall as the garage. I saw the weeds invading the previously carefully edged borders of the beds; the leggy red hibiscus that is crying to be cut back. I noted that the lemon grass should be trimmed so the new growth will dominate its shape for spring.

There is too much to do to prepare for Boston for me to be able to spend hours in the garden right now. I observed that, in many ways, I will miss spring, too.

Yet, there I sat with the pup we bought because our son has a tumor. Waiting for the little dog to throw up. We don't have a fenced yard, so when he's outside he requires continual attention. I am not gardening. I am not writing. I am missing seasons.

▶ What have you missed lately?

God, I know that missing seasons isn't the end of the world, but it makes me sad. And a bit scared. What else have I missed? Today, this moment, let me breathe in your comfort. I can't afford to miss you.

❧ The pansies died

The marigolds lived, but the pansies have died. Somewhere between my hiring a housekeeper, finalizing the lease for the Boston condo, ordering medical records, reviewing EOBs, doing a workshop in California, and taking Betsy, our younger daughter, on a spring-break jaunt to New Orleans, the pansies bit the dust.

As you might recall, my window boxes are in almost continuous need of watering. Earlier in this journey, I celebrated the miraculous fact that my marigolds were still getting watered in the midst of this trauma. Obviously, that is no longer the case.

I cannot remember the last time I watered them. I thought it was rainy enough this winter. Apparently not. Maybe the problem was that the season had changed to spring while my altered awareness remained stuck in winter.

In any event, my daughter and I noticed today that the pansies are dead—not dying, but dead. Tomorrow I will dig them up. Sadly, I won't plant anything in their place just yet. The boxes will lie fallow until we return from Boston.

They remind me of a time years ago when my husband and I had a fight over weedy flowerbeds. It was a particularly stressful time in our lives with his demanding job and my often overwhelming responsibility for the care of our three young children. He was upset because he had been told that you could tell the state of family life inside a home by the care of their landscaping outside.

In that moment years ago, I had boldly owned the unkempt state of our garden and said I was happy for anyone to know things weren't going so well inside. My response reflected the anger all too common in my soul in those years.

Today, I just feel sad. The pansies died. Oh, there will surely be other years with lovely window boxes. But not this spring. This spring is for tending to tumors, not window boxes. Now there's a thought, an odd but lovely image indeed: Here's to the tumor withering and dying just like the pansies died.

► In this season of challenge, what parts of your life are suffering from neglect, even unto death?

God, I am officially adopting these dead pansies as my prayer image for what I want to happen with this tumor. May it shrivel up, wither, and die.

❧ Opening the door to sweetness

I never had a sweet tooth until I married my husband, Robert.

Growing up, we had dessert only on special occasions. I certainly enjoyed it when we had it, but it never became a part of my daily routine. My husband, however, grew up in a very different atmosphere. His mother's favorite saying was "Life is short. Eat dessert first!" With the exception of breakfast, which was always accented with liberal amounts of homemade jelly and jam, she served dessert with every meal. That is, you had a precut serving at your place setting before the meal even began. She took her motto seriously!

As is always the case, once we married, we had some negotiating to do. Pretty quickly we settled on the idea of a "little something sweet" after most meals, a habit we've enjoyed now for twenty-five plus years.

This Lent I gave up sugar. I cannot tell you how many times I have silently blasted my husband in the last several weeks for ever introducing me to that "little something sweet." It would have been so much easier if I had never opened that door.

Or so I would like to think.

In this moment of wanting what I cannot (all right, choose not) to have, I would rather pronounce the very desire as evil than suffer this small measure of pain. How crazy is that? To be willing to forsake ever having dessert just so I won't feel this momentary ache and loss of pleasure?

I sense that in many areas I have made that kind of radically self-protective decision. I have refused to become emotionally vulnerable with trustworthy friends when someone has betrayed me. I have refused to even acknowledge my needs because they are not always met. I have refused to pray for my heart's deepest desire because I fear that God will say "no."

The challenges before me are clear: Will I enjoy the seven weeks in a lovely Beacon Hill condo though the only reason I am there is because our son has a brain tumor? Will I open my heart to this gracious gift for this unique moment and receive the comfort I long for? Will I dare to open the door to sweetness?

▶ Are there moments of sweetness you hesitate to embrace in the midst of your season of pain?

God, though this season has much bitterness, I want to taste your sweetness whenever and wherever I can. Please, God, keep my heart open.

♣ Synchronicities

As I have noted before, I just love synchronicities, those times when earthly things line up in heavenly ways. They speak to me of the Presence of God in the dailyness of my life. They feel like loving touches from an intimately creative Creator.

On this tumor journey, synchronicities have served as comforting affirmations along an often frightening path. I have noted a few along the way. Here are some that bring me special comfort at this stage of the journey:

> I met at least six women from Boston while I was in California at a conference on domestic violence.
>
> The picture that hangs over the dining room table in the Boston condo is the same image of a praying man that hung over my husband's grandparents' table and ours for many years.
>
> The dates we were given for treatment are perfectly sandwiched between Easter and our younger daughter's high school graduation, allowing us to be home for both.
>
> The Travel Channel had a special on Boston that a friend taped for us, allowing us to preview the city before we even arrive.
>
> We will be spending the forty days of Easter (liturgical churches really stretch the celebration) on Joy Street. Yes, that's really the name of the street. It is ever so easy to connect this season of resurrection with our much prayed-for season of healing.
>
> The condo living room is a large room with wooden floors, a wall of paned windows, and yellow light, just like the room I sketched from my dream.
>
> From the map, it looks like there's a Starbucks at the halfway point on our five-minute walk to the hospital. I love, maybe even need, good coffee.

I experience the reality of God's loving attention and intimate affection though each one of these synchronicities.

▶ Have you noticed any synchronicities along your path?

"God, you search out my path and my lying down, and are acquainted with all my ways." Psalm 139:3

❧ A pumpkin-pie-filled sinkhole

I readily admit it is an odd image. I woke up yesterday morning realizing that I had been dreaming about a pumpkin-pie-filled sinkhole. As the day went on, I slowly "unpacked" that image and realized it is a pretty good descriptor of my inner world right now. Let me explain.

The sinkhole. In my dream, my husband and I were sitting on the edge of our bed looking down into a sinkhole. Several objects from our home had already fallen into the pit: random shoes, books, and house parts including a long board like a two-by-four. Interestingly, I remembered that I have described this tumor journey as a sinkhole before: an unexpected, somewhat slow-motion disaster with the unique challenge of not quite ever being able to determine the full extent of the damage.

The pumpkin pie filling. Thanksgiving is my favorite holiday. There's something about the bounty of the harvest, the refreshment of cooler weather, and the gathering of friends and family around the call to give thanks that really works for me. It is also the only time of the year when I make pumpkin pie. I think my sinkhole was filled with pumpkin pie because I am experiencing the ambience of that holiday in the midst of this tumor journey. There is sweetness and bounty, a gathering of family and friends, and much, much giving of thanks.

The activity. At one point, my husband reached down into the pit (which was actually way farther down than he would be able to reach in the non-dream world) and picked up a board I knew to be nine feet long. He used it to attempt to plumb the depths of the sinkhole. His experiment was inconclusive. So is the outcome of this tumor journey. Will treatment be effective? Will there be side effects? Big ones? Small ones? No matter how hard we try, we do not yet know the depth of the sinkhole.

The emotion. Often, the emotional tone of a dream contains the strongest message of all for me. In the midst of an unplumbed sinkhole, there was no fear in this dream, only warmth and curiosity. I felt safe on my bed even while attentive to the reality of this encroaching sinkhole. I knew that eventually it might require us to relocate, to change our lives in significant ways, but even that thought brought more confidence of provision than anxiety.

As I have often said, I never know where comfort might come from. Today it came in the unlikely form of a pumpkin-pie-filled sinkhole.

▶ What unexpected sources of comfort have you encountered? Dreams? Friends? Helpful professionals? Music? Poetry?

Creator God, how soul-expanding it is to know your creativity through so many disparate expressions of comfort. Don't let me miss a single one!

❧ Rushing spring

I went shopping yesterday for an Easter dress. I decided that I wanted a yellow one.

I looked and looked and looked. Yellow is not an easy color for me to wear. It has to be a nice icy, pale yellow to look good with my skin. There were none to be found.

So, I broadened my search, simply looking for something I liked. I found a linen dress, a long, layered sleeveless A-line garment, white beneath and bright gray above. The gray is actually a woven fabric of black and white linen treads. The dress is uniquely styled and utterly comfortable.

Now, this may be a stretch for many of you, but shopping is often a tool God uses to help me grow in self-awareness. As a very intuitive woman, I often choose a garment to wear that reflects the state of my soul, sometimes surprising the conscious part of who I am.

I realized yesterday that in my intent to find yellow I was trying to rush spring. Though I am very hopeful for our son's complete healing, the reality is that this journey is still very much in a liminal space, much undetermined, very mixed in possibilities. I am living gray, not yellow. A part of me knew that all along. Seeing it in the dress, however, invited me to own this place of tension for a while longer.

When I met with my spiritual director, Catherine, last week, she told me that she so admired our amazing patience in all this. She spoke of how she has observed that we have refused to rush forward with treatment for the sake of relieving our personal tension. We have taken our time to do our homework and investigate and process each step along the way.

Though I was surprised by her observation that day, I sense that what she said was true, especially in this moment when I see myself moving away from that patience. Informed by my dress choice and buoyed by her encouragement, I take a deep breath, embracing once again this gray space in life, and begin to repent from rushing spring.

▶ Have you found yourself seeking to rush through certain parts of your journey? What insights, people, or experiences have helped you accept a slower pace?

God, though I long for the certainty of new life in spring, I want, even more so, to know the gift and wisdom of each season well lived.

"What if"

What if I were still working at the hospital? How could I possibly handle all this, too?

What if this tumor had not been discovered until Bob's eyesight had been lost or his major hormones shut down or he had a seizure?

What if he were newly married or without insurance?

What if we had found it when he was six or seven years old, with two other preschoolers at home?

What if we had heard about proton beam radiation after he had had standard radiation treatments or surgery?

What if he goes blind?

What if Bob has a seizure while it's just he and I in the Boston condo?

What if I have a hard time concentrating on editing the book?

The "What if" list feels endless.

Why in the world do I "What if" myself to death?

Though I am tempted to rail against the foolishness of engaging these unanswerable questions, the chaplain in me knows that all this "What if" energy is actually a form of healthy coping called anticipatory grief. Through the door of "What if," I am trying to internally prepare for possibilities, almost like the natural process of false labor preparing a woman to deliver a baby.

Of course, as with most coping mechanisms, I could overuse this "What if" business and get lost in all the anxiety. But, for now, I will choose to let it run its course, seeking its wisdom, refusing its compulsion, allowing healing for today to come in the form of "What if."

▶ How often do you play the "What if" game? Do you see it as helpful? Overused?

God, I sense that, ultimately, each and every "What if" needs to be surrendered to your hand and your wisdom.

Personhood and pain

Last week I was visiting with a friend I had not seen in a while. It was good to see Trisha but I was sad to hear that she was in such pain.

Her twenty-six-year-old daughter is really struggling with life. Unable to hold a job, she is jumping from relative to relative, friend to friend, blaming others, especially her mom, for all that goes wrong in her life. There is much pain on all sides of this equation that seems bound for disaster.

As Trisha was telling me about her situation, my friend made an interesting observation. She noted that this is not the hardest thing she has ever endured in her life but it is the most painful. She told me about the years she spent in an abusive marriage with her daughter's father. She noted, "It is so odd. Even with all I went through, I felt little pain. I think it's because in those days I didn't feel anything at all. I didn't know I could feel. I didn't even know I was a person."

There is a real connection between personhood and pain. I connected very strongly with what Trisha was saying. I, too, spent many, many years unaware of my personhood. As I have said before, I saw myself more as a machine than as a flesh-and-blood human being. In fact, I remember the very day I discovered my humanity.

My husband and I were loading a U-Haul trailer for our family's move back to Texas. We were winding up a year spent in Seattle for the purpose of graduate schooling for me. It had been a wonderful year and I was beyond sad to be leaving.

As we sought to stuff the metal frame of an old trundle bed into an already over-stuffed trailer, a sharp point from the frame sliced the skin on the lower part of my thumb.

I saw it happen. I watched the skin tear. I saw the blood begin to rise and fill the space. I knew, surprisingly for the first time really, that I was flesh and blood. I could be wounded. I could be torn and injured. I am not a machine but a person, a human person.

A person in pain.

Trisha hurts more now because she knows she is a person. I do, too. There is a real connection between personhood and pain.

▶ How painful has this challenging season been for you? How does it compare to past pain?

God, do I even dare to thank you for this pain? At least I know that I am alive.

✿ Prayer companions

I received an e-mail this morning from Lynn, a friend in London. She is heading out of town early to visit grandchildren for Easter and wanted to let me know that she is and will be praying for us as we go to Boston.

I am amazed by her awareness of our situation and her faithfulness to pray for us. It has been weeks since I sent out an update. I do not know much about this dear friend, having only spent time with her briefly at a conference more than a year ago, but I do know firsthand the sincerity and fervor with which she prays. She is a precious prayer companion on this journey.

Later, as I sat in church, God gave me another somewhat different kind of prayer companion. Better said, it is a written prayer to companion me on this next phase of our journey. In my youth, I had quite a lot of contempt for written prayers. But in recent years, I have developed a deep appreciation for these ancient words that speak time-tested wisdom.

I have a habit of praying through some of the collects or written prayers from the Book of Common Prayer as I wait my turn to receive communion. (As you may recall, I sit near the back of the church, so it can take a while.) Today I encountered a familiar prayer that stopped me. Prayers for family and personal life, number fifty-four, "for those we love."

Almighty God, we entrust all who are dear to us to Thy never-failing care and love, for this life and the life to come, knowing that thou art doing for them better things than we can desire or pray for; through Jesus Christ our Lord. Amen.

When I began to sense that these were words God was giving me for the next phase of our tumor journey, my first response was a polite and appropriately reverent, "No, thank you." The pianist played, *Jesus Loves Me* and *Oh, How He Loves You and Me.*

I don't want to pray these words. They give God way too much latitude. They give God permission to turn this thing in directions that I do not want it to go. They ask me to trust at a level that I do not want to trust. They seek to re-orient my very soul in disruptive and frightening ways.

The very presence of such resistance in my heart confirmed for me that, like it or not, these ancient and wise words are indeed my new prayer companion.

▶ What is your own internal response to the prayer above? Does it offer comfort? Incite resistance? Welcome new thought?

God, I know you love me. But sometimes, in hard times, I am just not sure I trust that love. I am not so sure I trust that I will still believe in your love if this journey goes in certain unwanted directions.

❧ Lending me hope

As we began our tumor journey, you may recall that I purchased a pendant. It is a piece of Venetian glass, a large bead, aqua in color with an inner silver core. I bought it as a celebration of my first book contract, but it soon became my prayer, a request to God that I would be able to see beauty in this journey.

And I have seen much beauty in many different arenas in our life together in these months; much of it recorded in this work. But, somewhere along the way, my vision for seeing beauty has begun to fade. I think it was around the time when I began to try to "ramp up" for this next phase of the journey and began confronting the detailed realities of this decision. About that time, I stopped wearing my pendant, without even thinking about what that choice reflected at my core.

Perhaps my friends could see my loss of hope. Perhaps they could sense how very heavy the burden of it all had begun to feel. One by one, they began to lend me hope through envisioning beauty for me.

One looked on the Web for nice places to live in Boston. Another called a friend there and sent me her contact information. She even sent me a card that specifically said her prayer for me was to see beauty! Yet another began to move toward raising money for our expenses with a fourth. They talked to us about restaurants, museums and baseball parks.

I was energized by their enthusiasm. When I hesitated, trying to "settle for less" once more, they pushed ahead with big dreams and wonderful plans. Even now, I struggle at times to imagine what the beauty will look like in Boston. My hope still feels like it is wearing a bit thin. Yet, they see it all with clarity and confidence. They are looking at calendars and planning dinner parties.

They have become one of the answers to my prayer; they are the beauty I long to see, even as they continue lending me hope.

► Who or what has offered you hope along the way?

God of hope, open my heart and grant me the courage to hope once more.

How can love be felt?

I use to think the message of the cross was all about justice. God sent Jesus to die on earth to pay the price for my sins so I would not need to bear that penalty. One of the reasons I enjoy a liturgical church is because I have the opportunity to receive communion at least weekly. That message of reconciliation through sacrifice is my very ground.

In recent years, though, the cross has come to have a message far more powerful for me than justice. Several years ago, I heard a pastor friend, William, say that the cross was more about love than about justice. As a Christian for many years, intuitively I felt that resonate with me, but I also knew that, at least on an intellectual level, I did not yet grasp what he was saying. But the notion remained.

Recently, I heard a radio spot that reported new brain research that proves we can work very effectively to solve problems even when we are not thinking about them consciously. That must have been what I did with this one because I don't remember when I began to understand what he was saying, I just know I do now.

For me, it's all wrapped up in the question: How can love be felt? You can feel it through affirmation, kind words, through gifts, through physical touch, and in many other ways. But the biggest test of love is sacrifice; the biggest proof is sacrifice that includes suffering. Yes, the cross is about justice, but more powerfully, *much* more powerfully, it is about love.

So, why is it that I so seldom will allow others to sacrifice on my behalf? Why do I refuse their love?

My friend Bonnie is in town. She said to me, "Can't you see that, over and over, your message in this is that giving to you is a gift for the giver?"

I struggle so to hold on to that thought. I am learning. I sense that this is one of those places in my heart that is being reshaped.

Perhaps I struggle because I am so stingy, struggling to give.

Perhaps my own heart is so stingy because I have refused to receive the love of others for far too long. I want to be loved. I need to be loved. I am learning to let myself be loved; otherwise, how can love be felt?

► How do you feel about being on the receiving end of giving?

God, as you and others seek to love me, help me learn to open my arms to graciously receive instead of raising them in protest.

❧ Stress points

The other day I had my third and final lenten massage. It is a tradition I began a number of years ago as a way of reminding myself of the delightful and freeing essence of repentance.

It has always amazed me how my body can hold stress in specific places. Once the therapist finds those places and releases the tension through massage, I feel it all over my body. There's a place in my foot that can relax my whole body, head to toe; a place in my shoulder that releases a rush of circulation to my arm; a point on my scalp that sets my neck and jaw muscles free. It is an amazing experience.

This week I realized that the same thing is true on a larger scale in my life. A few days ago, I hired Janie, a professional housecleaner, to clean my house. I wanted to line up someone to help my husband before we left and this was her training day. She did a fabulous job.

Now, I am gifted in many ways but housecleaning is not one of them. Yet, for some reason, having a clean house is very, very important to me. I have discovered that it is one of my stress points. Once Janie had worked her magic, I was amazed at the impact a clean house had on my soul.

The next day, I wrote and wrote and wrote, catching up on my vignettes within two days—all because my house was finally clean. The day after that, I faced the bills with an astonishing amount of energy and optimism.

Now, I do not really know why my body holds stress in certain places, nor do I completely understand why I have felt so freed to work on other things because my house was clean. I just know that both are true. Freedom in these particular spots in my life produces freedom elsewhere. The evidence of the Spirit's freer flow is there: more love, joy, peace, patience, goodness, kindness, faithfulness, gentleness, and self-control.

Rather than trying to analyze and judge and figure out these stress points, I want to seek to use this data to live more freely. As I write, I think of Lazarus being freed from his grave clothes. Jesus said, "Unbind him, and let him go."

Lord, unbind me. Let me go. Free me. Release my stress points.

▶ What are your stress points? What offers you more internal freedom?

O, God, you have searched me and known me; now free me, I pray.

⚘ Growing in grace

This was a grace-filled morning for me. As I mentioned before, my house was clean. My list of things to do today was actually doable. I wrote the vignette idea of the day this morning. I walked. It rained last night and cleared the air of pollen and refreshed the earth. It was in the seventies with a cool breeze and a bright, warm sun. As I sat on the patio at Starbucks sipping my decaf nonfat Venti Misto and editing the last twenty or so pieces I had written, a flock of cedar waxwings descended on the small newly planted trees nearby. My heart was full, as if I could feel it growing.

In the midst of that grace, even the enemies of the day were easily dealt with, the primary ones being guilt and fear. It is odd that in wonderful shining moments like these, evil seeks to diminish goodness by introducing random thoughts like:

Why are you feeling so good when your son has a brain tumor?

Sure, he's going to be fine, but what about the moms whose sons die of cancer?

Sure, people have been here for you this time, but what about all those other times when you hurt all alone?

Don't get your hopes up, this could all turn sour pretty quick.

Though these thoughts are in part true and my life must include space to wrestle with them, I sense that they come to me now not as wisdom but as tricks of evil, attempts to diminish the beauty and glory of this moment. I will not allow that today.

Today, I will stand in this grace, soak it in, delight in it, and let it grow me into the more wise and more beautiful woman I am becoming.

Today, I am growing in grace.

▶ Recall some grace-filled moments or days along your way. What people or places, experiences or insights allowed you to feel God's grace within and around you?

"But grow in the grace and knowledge of our Lord and Savior Jesus Christ. To him be the glory both now and to the day of eternity. Amen." 2 Peter 2:18

❧ Grievous connections

As we were singing a hymn this morning in church, I realized once again how deeply this tumor journey has penetrated my soul.

The song was an old familiar tune: *Amazing Grace*. The last stanza speaks of our life after death.

When we've been there ten thousand years
Bright shining as the sun
We've no less days to sing God's praise
Than when we've first begun.

As I was singing that verse, I realized with a start that I wasn't thinking of my own death, as I usually do, but my son's. In fact, in retrospect, I recognized that any time I've confronted the notion of death in the last few weeks, I've made the same internal association.

Now, I do not believe he is going to die from this tumor—at least I don't think I do. But something inside me thinks he's closer to death now than I am.

On some level in my soul, I am probably making lots of these kinds of connections, maybe even millions, all of which reflect my ongoing grief and concern. Only in rare moments like this one are those unconscious connections exposed.

I sense in this recognition God's invitation for me to extend compassion toward my own soul and my son's. If I am preoccupied in this way on some deep level, continually making these kinds of grievous connections, how much more so he must be making his own grievous connections.

▶ How and when have you become aware of your ongoing grief and pain that continually abide below the surface of your life? Have you responded to such awareness with greater self-compassion? Judgment? Impatience?

Heal me, O God, and I shall be healed. Save me, and I shall be saved.

❧ Jesus' peace

What exactly does the peace of Christ look like in real time? For years I thought of it in inhumane terms, defining peace as being unmoved by life around me. Having now given up my mechanistic identity and therefore concluded that it does *not* look like being unmoved, I have been on a quest for the last week or so to define it.

A few days ago, we arrived in Boston. In between initial appointments with doctors and never-ending MRIs and CAT scans, we began to try to settle into our condo. Though I had seen several pictures of this place and had heard great reviews from our leasing agent and the independent perspective of a friend, there was no substitute for seeing it myself. It feels like home.

I wondered to myself, "How can this be? It's someone else's house; someone I've never even met." We've rented condos at the beach before and they always felt like rented condos, not like this. Not like home.

Now this experience wasn't special because everything was perfect. The DSL had been disconnected. Someone had left a vase of long dead roses on the table. And the remote-controlled blinds were not working. Just like at home, my faithful husband set about solving these issues one at a time. Perhaps the imperfection was a part of the charm, a humanness of sorts, a connection with the ordinary.

I can rest here. I can do life here. Cook, watch TV, write, visit, shop, read. My stomach does not feel tight here. There is no sense of foreignness here. Or the need to be alert in a strange and unfamiliar place. Or a need to "adjust" to newness. I can be who I already am, and it works with this place. It all feels "in the flow" of my life rather than out of sync.

Perhaps that is the metaphor I've been watching for this week. Perhaps the peace of Christ is that sense that whatever comes my way is "in the flow" of my life: the good, the bad, or the ugly. That image assumes that I *will* be moved by life, moved and perhaps even redirected but not overwhelmed or interrupted.

Perhaps, the key to finding that peace is to learn to trust the river, to learn to ride the river rather than fight the river. Somehow, to learn the art of negotiating both my powerlessness and my power, my helplessness and my ability to influence my path. Living "in the flow"; living Jesus' peace.

▶ How do you define the peace of Christ? Has your current journey changed your definition?

"And let the peace of Christ rule in your hearts, to which indeed you were called in the one body. And be thankful." Colossians 3:15

The beauty of bend and sway

Today I took a long walk on Boston Common. It is early spring right now. The snow is gone and the landscape is barren. No bright winter snow. No golden orange fall leaves. No lush green summer hues. And no spring flowers. Not yet, at least.

There is, however, one bright spot amid the grays and browns: the yellow willow trees. I have had a love affair with willow trees for many years now. I love the way they bend and sway, gracefully and gently giving witness to even the slightest breeze. Even void of leaves, their soft form drew me toward them today.

A few years ago, I went on retreat to a monastery in Wisconsin, a place with several huge willow trees by a small glacier lake. I would sit for long hours under the trees in the cool fall air weaving wreaths of all sizes from the supple, golden fallen branches. It reminded me of joyous and sacred moments in my childhood when I made azalea perfume and purses or clothes out of huge leaves that grew on our neighbor's tree.

As I walked today, I picked up several yellow willow branches that had fallen. These fresh spring branches were especially malleable. As I gathered them and continued on my way, I enjoyed their soft, flexible feeling in my hand. They bend and sway so beautifully.

For days, I have been curious about my increased anxiety about this course of treatment for our son. Over and over I have asked myself, "What are you worried about? What exactly do you fear?" It isn't medical obstacles; we have tremendous support and the best care. It isn't loss; I know whatever the losses we may face, God's grace will allow us to grieve and heal. So, where is this anxiety coming from?

As I swish the willow from hand to hand with delight, I begin to hear the voice of God inviting me to live the beauty of bend and sway. Suddenly I know that my anxiety is rooted in my own inflexibility. The particular and inflexibly imagined future I had planned for myself and those I love might not be as I have planned it. It may not be as smooth as I desire.

God and the willow entice me to let go of my inflexibility and anxiety, to embrace and to live the beauty of bend and sway.

▶ Can you think of any particularly inflexible dreams or visions about your future that have been threatened by your recent pain and loss? Do you sense God inviting you to bend and sway?

God, open my eyes and my heart to new, and perhaps even greater, visions of beauty you are offering me and those I love. I want the wisdom of these willows.

❧ Little one

I realized the other day that I am developing a new relationship with fear in my life. For many years, fear has been a core struggle of mine. We all struggle with something. I battle fear.

A number of years ago, my spiritual director, Catherine, invited me to hug my fear rather than fight it. Her suggestion startled me at first. How could I have compassion on something that seemed to be so limiting and destructive in my life? Her suggestion began an on-and-off journey for me that became more "on" than "off" with the discovery of Bob's tumor.

Last fall, as we visited again about fear, I realized that when I am afraid, my personal image of myself is that of a small waif of a girl huddled in the corner of a dark, imposing library. Once again, Catherine invited me to care for that little child with compassion rather than shaming her for being afraid.

Though I felt that I had a bit more understanding of what she was saying, I continued to struggle with having compassion on a trait I had loathed within myself for so long.

Out at the monastery one day not long after my meeting with Catherine, I heard Brother John greeting his precious cat, Schnurrli ("little purrer" in German). With more love than words on a page can contain, he reached down to gently stroke her eagerly arching back as he said, "little one." Now, that was not a new scene for me. I had heard him speak to her that way many, many, many times before, but for some reason this time his greeting struck me differently.

Suddenly, I had an image of the loving and nurturing heart of God toward that fearful little girl huddled in that corner, the "little one." Through the love and sheer affection in John's voice, I understood God's compassion toward my fear.

So, my relationship with fear is changing. When I feel like that frightened child huddled in the corner of the dark, imposing library, I no longer shame her for being afraid. Instead, I hear the voice of God reaching toward me, full of love and sheer affection, saying once again, "little one."

▶ Do you have an image of yourself when you are afraid? Have you felt like a child at any point in this journey? Do you respond with judgment? Contempt? Compassion?

Christ, you say to bring the little children to you. I suppose that applies even if they happen to be housed in the body of my grown-up self. Teach me to extend that same compassionate welcome.

🌿 To witness transformation

I decided that I am really glad we made it to Boston before spring had sprung. The trees are still barren, the grass brown, and though the foliage and bulbs are shooting up everywhere, blooms are few and far between.

I want to see it happen. I want to witness spring unfold. I want to savor every moment of this healing and restoring yearly rhythm. And I know that to witness it all means spending some time with the cold, the dreary, and the barren.

I wish I could say I had such wise and willing vision for my children. As I was picking dead leaves off a vine that has begun to sprout on our little bit of a Boston patio, I realized that I needed to do some "dead leaf picking" of another sort.

As I noted in a previous vignette, I have recently realized that I have some pretty inflexible dreams and images of what I want my life, and the lives of those I love, to look like. This tumor journey has not just threatened those dreams, I am coming to realize that it has awakened me to the realization that they have already died a very natural death.

Today, for the first time, I am facing how very shallow my vision has been for my children. I not only want comfort for them, I want a smooth ride. I want them to acquire character magically, without the suffering so intrinsic to that formation process. I don't want them to have tumors and accidents and rejections and failures. I don't ever want them to know winter.

Yet they must. If they are to become the transformed and transforming people I so want them to be, they must. I am confident (and comforted) that the God who loves them more than I has seen to it that they will not miss winter.

The real question is will I be willing to be with them in their suffering? Will I try again and again to undo what God has done? Will I rescue, deny and not allow their pain and grief? It is one thing to learn to embrace winter personally; it is a whole other thing to embrace it in the lives of my children.

As I pick each dead leaf, I let go old dreams, making way for new ones. I so want to witness transformation.

▶ How do you respond when those you love are hurting?

Lord, help me to be with my children in winter, in the cold, dreary, and barren places.

✿ Someone else's garden

I have found it absolutely delightful to tend someone else's garden this spring. Now "tending" is probably a generous description of what I done thus far, removing a few dead leaves and old branches. Probably better said, I have been observing.

Every morning I go out to see what new spot of green has broken ground. As the sun is warmer and warmer, in the sky longer and longer, these hidden wonders are responding each according to their own intrinsic rhythm and in their own special way.

I don't yet know what any of the blooms will look like. I recognize the shape of a hyacinth but have no clue about its color. The same with what looks to be a tulip leaf. You can bet I will eagerly anticipate each revelation with excitement and celebration.

As I was brushing dirt away from one newly appearing shoot today, I thought, "Tending someone else's garden is a lot like life—you never know what's going to come up next. Why is it that I don't respond in the same optimistic way to life's uncertain reality as I do to this one?" Perhaps the problem is not simply the uncertainty. Maybe there is a deeper issue at work.

Perhaps it is a matter of trusting the goodness and intent of the gardener. I trust that the owner has not planted poison ivy or thorns. I anticipate only good and am not afraid at all. Though certainly there will be weeds, I am confident they will be manageable.

Things are different with this tumor journey. Do I really trust that God will never give me more in life than I can endure? Do I believe that for my children? Do I trust life's Gardener?

How different my life will look if (when?) I choose to live the uncertainty of my life with the same delightful anticipation, wonder, and celebration I have found as I tend someone else's garden.

▶ Has your current pain made you more aware of the uncertainty in life? How do you respond to that uncertainty?

God, in your goodness, you send rain and sunshine to all. Plant my life in the reality of your generosity that my heart may bring forth the fruit of trust.

❧ The personality factor

Medical science is a very human system. Though few of us want to admit that, it is so very true. We would rather believe it is simple mathematics: one plus one equals two. And, in fact, some aspects of medicine are that cut and dried. But only some.

Our situation is not among the "cut and dried." From the very beginning, we have seen that it is an area of varying opinions.

Now, there is science that plays into all this. But it's not exactly the one plus one kind. It is statements like, "Overall, the treatment will produce preservation of vision," and "Radiation has been proven effective against this kind of tumor for many years."

There are many more statements like, "Every tumor is unique." And, "We don't know how your particular tissues will respond." And, "Odds are low but we can't exactly give you numbers. There just aren't enough cases out there that have been followed." Some say maximum impact on tissues will be seen at six months to a year, some say eighteen months, some say years down the road. No one knows what the impact will be sixty years after treatment because the technology has just been around twenty years. We plan on Bob having a good *long* life!

So, what does all this have to do with personality? One of the first surgeons we saw mentioned that treatment choices were often a function of personality. He, for example, would choose surgery. Even at a higher risk of damage, at the end of the day, he would know what was preserved and what he had lost definitively. He had no tolerance for uncertain outcomes.

Thankfully, he was wise enough to see that others could make equally legitimate choices depending on their personalities.

The problem for me is that our son has one personality and I have another. He handles uncertainty very well. I do not. He copes well with risk. I do not.

Thankfully, I know this decision is his.

Unfortunately, that doesn't make learning to live with it easier for me as I struggle, because of the personality factor.

▶ How has your particular personality made your journey more difficult? Has it also been helpful in other ways? How have others differed in their responses?

"My frame was not hidden from you, when I was being made in secret, intricately woven in the depths of the earth. Your eyes beheld my unformed substance." Psalm 139:15–16

❧ Oh ye of little faith

That's me all right. A woman of little faith.

Bob goes for his first treatment tomorrow morning and I am anything but full of faith in this moment.

In the midst of my anxiety, I remember all the wonderful graces we have encountered along this path:

The gentleness of the path.

Good doctors.

Bits of bright sky beyond the tangled and dark woods.

Amazing technology.

A favorable pathology report.

Decisions by journey.

Generous, generous, generous friends.

A wonderful place to live.

Many and varied moments of comfort.

God has met me at every turn, so why, oh, why do I doubt now?
Oh ye of little faith.
That's me all right. A woman of little faith.
The possibilities of big losses seem so real. Though small, very real.
Scripture says that faith as small as a mustard seed can move mountains.
Perhaps the smallness of my faith is not so important.
Perhaps the important thing is what, or rather in Whom, my faith abides.
Perhaps I can rest even as I own my new title of "Oh ye of little faith."

▶ Has your journey challenged your faith? When has it felt large? When small?

I believe, God, help my unbelief.

Regret

I looked it up this morning. It comes from the French word, "to weep." It means "to weep again" or to "re-weep."

I looked it up because last night I realized that regret is a big deal in my life. Fear of regret has been the reason I have made many limiting decisions. One of my biggest hesitations around this decision for radiation treatment is, "Will Bob come to regret this decision in future years? Will I regret not 'forcing' or at least trying to persuade him to take a more 'conservative' course?"

The answer to the first question is pretty clear: Bob lives his life with very few regrets. It's just not something he seems to struggle with in any area. His dad is the same way.

This is *my* issue.

Interestingly, several years ago when our older daughter, Jenna, was deciding on a university, I refused to let her make a decision on the basis of avoiding regret. She was choosing between a small school and a huge one. She said initially that she would go to the larger one because she was afraid she would regret it if she did not.

I called it an "un-decision." I insisted she make a selection based on the merits of the schools, on what each offered her that was uniquely good for her. Not on the basis of a fear of regret.

Even though I imposed that requirement on my daughter, I struggle myself.

It is intriguing now to think of my fear of regret as a fear of "weeping again."

As one who sees herself so given to the healthy processing of grief, perhaps I'm a bit deluded. Might I be afraid of a future loss and its accompanying grief? Maybe I am not as confident in the healing process of grief as I thought. Maybe I just don't like pain. Perhaps there is more grief work to be done, exposed this day by a new definition of "regret."

▶ Are you struggling with regret or allowing the fear of regret rather than vision to shape important decisions?

Oh, God, give me the courage to face life without a fear of weeping or even weeping again.

❧ Shifting gears

Today we begin shifting gears. This is Bob's first day of radiation treatment and I am finally convinced that the decision has been made and this is something that we are going to do.

Now, you may have assumed that since we've signed a very expensive lease for seven weeks and been in Boston over a week that the decision was finalized long ago. And I think that was the case for my husband and son. But for me, the decision mode ends today. This feels a bit like the last few minutes before the bride walks down the aisle: It ain't really decided till all parties show up at the altar. Or in this case, the proton beam machine.

This all seems almost anticlimactic. At least I hope it will be that way. I am praying for a blessedly routine course of treatment and many blessedly normal years to come.

I brought my pastels with me today. My plan is to do a mandala each day as a form of prayer, imaging healing. Last night as I packed my bag, I was doubtful that I would be able to do anything creative at all in this moment. I was so full of anxiety the thought of putting pastel to paper seemed beyond my capability.

But this morning, things are better inside me, more settled. It feels as if I really am shifting gears.

"What happened in the night?" I wonder. I was somewhat restless but awoke ready and not feeling particularly weary.

I think it may be all the prayers. I certainly didn't reason myself to this point. I didn't shame myself here. I think it may be the many, many, many prayers being offered today on our behalf that are making a way for my soul to begin shifting gears.

▶ Have there been points along your own journey when you have "shifted gears"? How have you negotiated the changes?

God, thank you for the freedom to simply "be" where I am, without judgment or shame. God, help me to be present to those around me.

🌿 At rest

I know I am at rest when:

The thought of creating excites me.

I wear skirts, not pants.

I breathe deeply without even thinking about it.

My body bends and moves flexibly and with full extension.

I get hungry and eat only then.

I don't overeat.

I crave silence, not noise.

I stretch often.

I rarely feel the need to nap.

I only watch the news once a day.

I laugh easily and from my belly.

I don't think much about money, and when I do, the thoughts are matter-of-fact thoughts.

I read.

I initiate sex with my husband.

I do not crave sweets.

I spend less time in cyberspace.

I take long hot baths.

Though it feels miraculous that I experience it at all right now, I find myself moving in and out of being at rest.

► What do you notice about your own patterns of being at rest? Have you found that place lately?

"In returning and rest you shall be saved; in quietness and in trust shall be your strength." Isaiah 30:15

❧ "How is it…?"

How is it that brain tumor treatment for us means spending the best part of the spring in Boston, a three-minute walk from the Common?

How is it that our son does not have pain with his tumor?

How is it that his tumor is slow-growing?

How is it that his vision has been preserved even with the tumor pressing three sides of his optic chiasm?

How is it that we are living in a beautiful condo on Beacon Hill, just around the corner from former presidential candidate John Kerry?

How is it that I have the money to take our daughter to see *Phantom of the Opera*?

How is it that I get notes, calls, and e-mails from friends and family on a daily basis, evidence of the hundreds of prayers being said on our son's behalf?

How is it that we have flown back and forth to Boston twice and not paid a dime?

How is it that grace, so unearned and undeserved, fills our lives with unspeakable richness in the midst of the most challenging time our family has yet to face?

Grace is beautiful.

Grace is unpredictable.

Grace is beyond management.

Grace is needed.

Grace is rooted in love.

Grace is a gift.

Grace leaves me amazed and forever asking, "How is it…?"

▶ How have you experienced grace along your journey?

Amazing grace. How sweet the sound, God. How very sweet.

✥ Small connections

I was home less than a week to see Betsy off to her senior prom, but in that time I had so many opportunities for life-giving small connections with those who love me.

Drew brought over stew.

Jacob called to invite Betsy and me to a crawfish boil.

Emily scheduled a writers' group when I was home.

Elizabeth did the same with my Sacred Circle group.

And Paula with a women-in-ministry lunch.

I got to be a part of a workday for Amma's House, an organization of which I am a board member.

I was present for a band concert for Betsy and viewed a photographic exhibit at the mall where she won three awards.

Jill and Iris, Karen and Jim, Theresa and Leslie, the list could go on and on of those who specifically asked me about Bob and told me of their continuing prayers.

I got a hug from Madison.

Carol affirmed that I am not crazy to enjoy Boston, even if we are there for brain tumor treatment!

Max said, "Keep the updates coming."

Sarah agreed to take pug Gary for several more days of doggy daycare, actually more like doggy preschool since she's been teaching him to sit and stay!

I enjoyed Evening Prayer with the monks.

My soul was refilled, refreshed, and made new through these many and various small connections.

▶ What small or large connections with supportive people are sustaining your journey?

Thank you, God, for the gift of those who suffer with me. "If one member suffers, all suffer together with it." 1 Corinthians 12:26

❧ Answers to questions I could not ask

Through many years of occasional travel, I have discovered that seemingly random airplane seating assignments are sometimes moments of "divine appointment." Such was the case this last week as I flew back to Boston after spending time in Texas.

I was seated next to a young man who is blind. Aaron has been legally blind since birth, totally blind since the age of seventeen. He lives in Boston and works as an instructor in a rehabilitation program for the blind.

As soon as I discovered that I was seated next to a young man who happened to be blind, my mind was flooded with questions. Questions looming large for months just below my level of consciousness. Questions I could not ask for fear of inviting "negative thinking" into my world. Questions I think God knew I needed to ask.

I tried to be polite and not overwhelm this kind gentleman with my fears and concerns. Slowly I inquired about his life.

He showed me his latest gadget: an iPod-like device that allowed him to download books or any scannable text into his computer, then have it read to him by new voice technology. He spoke of the revolutionary freedom he has now that the Internet and voice technology give him access to an unlimited amount of information.

He spoke of e-mail and how some of the people he converses with have no idea he is blind. He talked about choosing to live in Boston, where efficient mass transit makes his life easier. He talked about a life filled with friends and family and meaningful work.

I watched him graciously ask for help, such as an escort after landing. And he even more graciously received help he did not really need as a flight attendant insisted on pouring his beverage. I was amazed by his acceptance of his blindness. Through this brief encounter, I could imagine a rich and satisfying and good life available to my son no matter what happens.

Yet as I looked out the window of the airplane and reveled in the beauty of the coastline, I was overwhelmed with sadness that I could not share such beauty with Aaron. Still, even in the sadness, I thanked God for these answers to questions I could not ask.

▶ What are your most urgent questions at the moment? Are there some you hesitate to ask?

God, even before the word, or question in this case, was on my tongue, You knew it completely. Psalm 139:4

❧ Practicing disinterest

About two weeks into our Boston venture, Bob asked me to simply become disinterested in him.

I had not realized how my interest had been impacting him—becoming a burden more than a support.

Now, it may simply be that he doesn't want to deal with his own emotions around this tumor and treatment. And my willingness to be more open about my process makes him uncomfortable.

Or it may just be that I am being a pain as an over-concerned, over-anxious mom.

After recovering from a few minutes of indignant "How dare he!" I realized how important it was for me to listen to his request. The reason for his request did not really matter. The critical thing was for me to try to adjust myself to be less of a burden to him emotionally.

Now, there's no way to actually *be* disinterested in my son: that's just not what moms *do*. I can, however, choose to not expose him to my interest. I can practice being disinterested.

The first thing I did was leave town to visit a friend in Vermont for the weekend. Bob had a friend coming to visit so he wouldn't be alone. And my friend had really wanted me to visit. Bob's request was just the push I needed to get me going.

Since then, I've discovered that the easiest way to avoid over-interest in Bob is to become interested in other things available to me.

So…

Yesterday while our daughter Betsy was here to accompany him to his treatment, I had lunch with a friend. While Bob's brain was being zapped, I was eating balsamic fig and prosciutto pizza and riding Swan Boats in the Public Garden.

I am planning a trip to Cape Cod in a few weeks to discuss my book with a seminary professor who has invited me to her home. I am practicing disinterest.

▶ Has your over-concern impacted anyone around you negatively? How did you respond?

God, I'm trying here. But I really need your help to figure out how to walk this line. Once again, help me see what love looks like here.

❧ Blessedly routine

During my years as a chaplain, I often prayed for patients just before medical treatment of some kind: surgery, chemo, radiation, tests. Many times, my prayer was that the procedure be "blessedly routine."

I see the art and practice of medicine as a miraculous healing tool in the hand of God. A tool that has been developed and honed with careful science and research. A tool that relies on what it knows and often hesitates to admit how little it can really predict or control the human body.

Even when the treatment is for a burdensome diagnosis like cancer or heart disease, when the course of medical care goes according to plans and predictions, we are usually pleased.

Bob's biopsy was supposed to be routine. It was not. I was not pleased.

So, it is a bit more of a challenge to pray that these treatments will be "blessedly routine" and really expect it to happen.

Nevertheless, that has been my prayer…and thus far, our experience.

Historically, I have not been a person with a great deal of appreciation for the routine. I love the new and novel, the unusual and exceptional, those things that challenge the norm, the *more* of life.

Yet, I am discovering a new appreciation for the normal, the ordinary, the typical even as I continue to pray that this treatment course will be blessedly routine.

▶ Where have you found comfort in "blessedly routine" outcomes?

God, I never thought I would say it, but thanks for every minute of this utterly dull series of treatments. May they continue to be a complete bore.

✣ Better things

I don't know if you remember my prayer companion I wrote about a while back. Last night at Mass, as is my practice, I opened my Book of Common Prayer to page 831 and prayed again these visionary words: *Almighty God, we entrust all who are dear to us to Thy never-failing care and love, for this life and the life to come, knowing that thou art doing for them better things than we can desire or pray for; through Jesus Christ our Lord. Amen.*

I realized that I struggle particularly with the phrase "better things." In those words, I realized the stark limitations of my love for my children.

I want good things for them as long as those good things don't make them hurt. I don't want the "better things" of God.

I am wise enough to know that this pain-free kind of love, my kind of love, is short-sighted and ultimately destructive.

I am thankful that God loves them more than I do.

The trick is to not get in the way of that Divine love, to not seek to save them from what God allows in their lives: pain, disappointment, grief, loss, challenges, opportunity, even blessing.

The prayer strikes at my heart again when it notes that I cannot even *desire*, much less *pray* for, these "better things." My vision is so limited.

Lord, save these precious ones from my blindness, my feeble love. Love them more.

The prayer is centuries old. Maybe other parents have realized the stark limitations of their love for their children.

Maybe other parents struggle with "better things."

▶ Do your prayer intentions for those you love resemble the "better things" of God? Or do you, like me, suffer from short-sightedness?

Thank you, God, for loving them more. More than I can even imagine. Today, for some reason, that thought brings me comfort more then makes me afraid.

🌿 For the comfortless

Perhaps it's my experience as a chaplain. Perhaps it's my desire to run from being present to my own life. Perhaps it's my penchant for "big picture" perspective.

For some reason, as I process this experience, I am ever mindful of those whose suffering looks different from mine. Particularly, those who suffer without comfort.

The question arises for me: Are they really without comfort in this world or does it just look like they are?

As I look at my own life, I believe that there are many times when I have chosen to suffer without the comfort offered. I was too afraid to admit my need, too frightened of that kind of vulnerability, too scared to be open enough to receive.

Comfort was available. I just couldn't access it.

Couldn't or wouldn't?

I do not know the answer to that question.

But does it really matter? The fact remains that I was comfortless.

It would be utterly convenient to believe that comfort is available to all, and that if we do not experience it, it is because we choose not to.

Convenient but pointless.

Through this tumor journey, I am experiencing the many faces of comfort. I am learning to admit my pain, my grief, and my need. I am learning to receive. And I am comforted in my suffering.

But never far from my thoughts are those who do not know comfort.

Those to whom it is not available. Those who will not or cannot (who cares which it is) access what may or may not be offered.

I ache for myself.

I ache for Bob. But even more so, I ache for the comfortless.

▶ Do you consider yourself to be without comfort? Do you know others who are?

God, please comfort those who need to know your touch. Open hearts. Bring hope and peace, compassion and healing presence to all who weep tonight.

❧ So what do you expect?

The challenge of the day: So what do you expect?

The question of the hour: So what do you expect?

The current work of God in my life: So what do you expect?

Though most of my friends and acquaintances experience me as a positive person, I've come to recognize that I'm really not. I am quite the pessimist, always expecting and preparing for the worst.

Such "negative thinking" is, at least in part, simply the overuse of a positive penchant for planning. A critical part of effectual planning is anticipating bad things and arranging life so that you avoid those hazards.

I, however, take this to the extreme, seeking to banish all grief and pain, loss and harm from my life and the lives of those I love. With that goal in mind, I am disproportionately aware of hazards around me. And there are many. Thus, the pessimism.

I sense within this tumor journey God's invitation to let go of my fearful and negative expectations.

God wants me to expect goodness and abundance rather than evil, abandonment, and scarcity. Even in the *midst* of pain and loss, to expect grace, comfort, and provision.

Now, I don't think God is as interested in the power of positive thinking as much as reshaping what I believe about the God I serve.

My negativity says that ultimately I do not trust God's ever mindful, ever effectual love to be very loving or to be very good.

Will I ever grow up? Will I ever learn to trust this God who has carried me every step of the way? Will I ever begin to expect goodness and abundance?

My greatest fear is that all the miraculous grace and provision of this tumor journey will wash over me yet again, leaving me unchanged. I am afraid that my hard heart will forget, yet again, this abundantly evident goodness of God.

"So what do you expect?"

▶ What do you find yourself expecting these days? Goodness? Trauma? Provision? Abandonment? Grace? Grief? All of the above?

"Create in me a clean heart, O God, and put a new and right spirit within me."
Psalm 51:10

The gift of exhaustion

I knew I was simply exhausted when the second cup of coffee, Starbucks' Bold Sumatra no less, did not help.

We had an early treatment time, 8:30 AM. As I rolled out of bed at 7:30 and put my coffee on, I felt intensely weary. Two hours later when we returned from the treatment, I was just as tired, in spite of the two cups of highly caffeinated beverage I had fruitlessly consumed.

I told Bob that I was going back to bed. I even put my pajamas back on. That's how very tired I was.

Napping on and off most of the morning, I was just conscious enough to wonder about my extreme fatigue. Logically speaking, there seemed to be little justification. After all, what do I do all day? Emotionally speaking, the reasons were obvious.

For the last month, I've been in flux: transitioning to Boston, transitioning to a treatment schedule a week later, going back to Beaumont for the prom, then back to Boston with visitors.

This was our second day of simple routine. My body and soul knew that now was the time to collapse.

So collapse I did. In recent years, I have learned that it does little good to fight my exhaustion on a day like today. In fact, I've come to see the extremity of such moments as a gift: My body simply stops so my soul has time to catch up.

Sometime just before noon, I managed to dress once again and walked the few minutes to St. Paul's Cathedral across the Common. I had discovered yesterday via the Internet that they have a noon Mass.

The group was small: four women, one of whom, Winifred, was presiding. After Mass, Winnie invited me to have lunch with two of the three who had a habit of moving from the communion table to the lunch table.

As I visited with these hospitable women, I found myself fighting back tears more than once. My fatigue was easy to admit because it was so evident, unavoidable really. Through the door of my vulnerability, I experienced their comfort, unexpectedly discovering yet another gift of exhaustion.

▶ Have you encountered exhaustion along the way? How have you responded?

"O God, you are my God, I seek you, my soul thirsts for you; my flesh faints for you, as in a dry and weary land where there is no water." Psalm 63:1

✣ Listening to what is

It is a chief tenet of the Serenity Prayer…but not my strong suit.

"Help me accept the things I cannot change."

I have ideas, *lots* of ideas, about how life is supposed to work.

One of those ideas was about how ideal it was going to be to edit my first book while I had all this time on my hands in Boston. Though even that choice was an editor's schedule-imposed delay in the original plan (to have that job done before we left for Boston), it was a scenario I could live with.

Well, we are halfway through our time and the process has still not yet begun. I am beginning to panic.

I have committed to working at my other part-time job (relief chaplaincy) for the two months following our return to Texas. Working twenty hours a week at that job *and* editing under a close deadline is not my idea of fun, especially with our three kids in and out all summer. Just the thought of it pushes all my "I hate to be overwhelmed" buttons *big* time.

"Help me accept the things I cannot change."

This is one of those things. As a first-time author, I have precious little clout. From what I've heard through the grapevine, the editor who keeps putting me off is very good at what she does. I've communicated my schedule to her more than once. She is aware. I have done all I can.

My laid-back son says he's enjoying watching me squirm.

I've decided that my best defense against rank insanity (or at best irritating frustration), is offense: Rather than fighting what isn't, I am beginning to listen to what is.

Today, for example, "What is" was exhaustion. So I rested. (I shudder to imagine how I would have sought to push through my fatigue if I had had an assignment from my editor!) Today, I met two lovely, hospitable women who cared for my soul. Today, I read some in a new book that a friend from home sent me. Today, I took a walk in the park and wrote three vignettes. Today, thankfully, I began listening to what is.

▶ To what extent are you currently accepting things you cannot change and "listening to what is" and to what extent are you fighting it?

"God, grant me the serenity to accept the things I cannot change; the courage to change the things I can; and the wisdom to know the difference."

🌿 It always comes

Boston is in bloom. As I walked through the park today, evidence of spring was everywhere I turned. Everywhere I looked, I was reminded that spring always comes.

A three-year-old ballerina in a fluffy pink tutu twirled in the grass.

The red tulips were in full bloom.

There were tiny crabapples on the tree by the bridge.

The birds were louder than the traffic.

The pink tulips were in full bloom.

A young woman in a black suit and heels walked by with her eyes closed and a smile on her lips as she savored the warm sunshine.

Another sat cross-legged on the lawn busily writing.

A few short weeks ago, I would play the game of walking beneath the few trees that were blooming. Now, almost all the trees have some evidence of new green.

The yellow tulips with orange edges were in full bloom.

The pale pink saucer magnolia blossoms were drifting to the ground, released to carpet status as small green leaves pushed them off their high perches.

Did I tell you the lavender tulips were almost in full bloom?

Spring always comes. Sometimes early. Sometimes late. But it always comes.

To forget that fact would be foolish and unthinkable.

How is it then that I forget the goodness of God that always comes just like spring? Sometimes early, sometimes late. But it always comes.

▶ What season are you in? At this moment, is it easy or hard to remember that spring always comes?

"For now the winter is past, the rain is over and gone. The flowers appear on the earth; the time of singing has come." Song of Songs 2:11–12

❧ Open wide

I've been talking with some friends about my struggle to expect goodness from God. One sent me this verse this morning: "Open your mouth wide and I will fill it" (Psalm 81:10).

It reminded me of a children's song my daughters loved to sing in preschool (and still do on occasion!).

"If all of the raindrops were lemon drops and gumdrops, oh what a day this would be. I'd stand outside with my mouth open wide, Ah, ah-ah, ah, ah-ah, ah, ah-ah, ah. If all of the raindrops were lemon drops and gumdrops, oh what a day this would be."

Without the visual and sound effects of adorable, wispy-ringleted preschoolers with mouths wide open as they enthusiastically sing the "ah-ahs," I'm not sure I can give you the whole picture, but maybe you can imagine how cute it might be.

"Open your mouth wide and I will fill it."

What a challenging verse this is. In our world where shootings and tumors, car accidents and marital infidelity, alcohol addiction and layoffs happen on a daily basis, God invites us to open wide.

Not all the raindrops are lemon drops and gum drops.

But what option do I really have? If I shut myself off and refuse to let anything in, the good or the bad, I will die of starvation.

Not all the raindrops are lemon drops and gumdrops, but God promises that some are. God promises to fill me with good things.

Those words remind me of communion. As I eat bread and drink wine, I fill my life with both the suffering and resurrection love of Jesus' life.

Not all of his raindrops were lemon drops and gumdrops either.

In the end, goodness won. Sweetness prevails as an ever-lingering aftertaste of the gospel. A new invitation to expect goodness: Open wide.

▶ Do you find yourself opening wide or clenching your jaw in anger and fear?

God, I want to taste and see that you are good. Give me the courage to open wide and drink deeply from life.

❧ Pondering providence

As I was walking back from the park today, I began to wonder about the providence of God and this tumor journey.

We saw the neuro-endocrinologist again today to get the results of Bob's bone density and lab tests. Everything looked pretty good except for the bone density of his spine. Our twenty-three-year-old son has osteoporosis, thinning bones, in his spine. Actually, they aren't really thinning; they just never reached their full density as he grew due to the low levels of hormones. From what she said, she feels they are pretty fragile at the moment.

Thankfully, this is an issue easily remedied by several months on a weekly medication that will boost his bone density. Thereafter, the supplemental hormones he's already taking will do the rest.

The interesting thing is that two years ago he had a bad skiing accident. As he was changing runs at a ski resort in Colorado, he hit an icy patch and lost control of his skis, eventually hitting a stump with his rump just before kissing a tree with his head. Though he ended up with a severe flesh wound in an embarrassing location that took months of careful care to heal, he was otherwise unharmed.

Undoubtedly, the bone in his spine was thin even then. It is amazing that he did not break something important—like his spine.

I am thankful.

The other interesting connection we made was that if they had done a CAT scan or an MRI to verify the extent of any head injury (which thankfully his symptoms did not warrant), they would have found the tumor then.

It is impossible to know if an earlier diagnosis would have made any difference.

I do know that the same force that protected the spine did not reveal the tumor.

Maybe both were happenstance. Maybe they weren't. In any event, the possibilities find me pondering providence.

► Do you connect the idea of providence and your current suffering? Do you believe in it? If so, do you see it as a hindrance? Help? Both?

Here I am again God, asking some pretty unanswerable questions. Will I ever understand how the world works? Will I ever have the answers I seek? Does it even matter?

❧ The place of inspiration

In general, Episcopalians are very serious about beauty and about the importance of architecture. Boston Episcopalians are no exception. One of the delights of being here for me has been worshipping in a variety of beautiful Episcopal churches. Amazingly, there are five within a short walk of Beacon Hill. Tonight I went to Trinity Church.

I especially enjoy their Sunday evening service. They have a habit of gathering the large crowd around the beautiful, circular altar space for communion. We see the elements of Jesus' body in bread and wine as we encounter him in the faces of his body the church.

We stand in concentric circles under an elaborate dome, surrounded by carefully chosen, loving, nurturing words of God painted on the walls at our backs. In the most central place behind the altar is the reminder, "God is love." Light shines brightly through the stained glass windows above. The turquoise and the bright yellow inspire me most.

Each time I've gone, I have come away inspired once again. Somehow, I don't tend to anticipate that I will feel so encouraged by this simple choice to go to church and worship with people I do not know. Yet, somehow, I always am.

I like the word inspiration. The medical usage of the word best pictures for me the spiritual sense: to breathe in. A breath of fresh air comes my way, received and savored. The stuff of new life.

I don't know what it is about this place: the quiet, the sense of the sacred, the beauty, the positive energy, the familiarity of the liturgy. This place of inspiration gathers my soul. By the end of the hour, I feel as if the scattered pieces of my life have once again fallen into place. No problems have been solved or hurts healed, I simply have a greater sense of wholeness and the air I need to keep going. More often than not, I've also jotted a few notes on soon-to-be-written vignettes as well, thoughts first born in a place of inspiration.

▶ Where are your places of inspiration, life, and hope? Where can you breathe most deeply?

"O Lord, I love the house in which you dwell, and the place where your glory abides."
Psalm 26:8

❧ I think I may be getting sick

When I was eight years old, I went off to Girl Scout Brownie camp for a week. It was my first time ever to be away from home without my parents. I had looked forward to it for months. And I absolutely hated every minute of it.

I remember sitting on the steps outside my cabin fighting back tears. There was a sick taste in my mouth and an unsettled feeling in my gut.

My teenage counselor was oh-so-compassionate but she really couldn't help. She took me to the nurse because I thought I was really sick. And I was; I was homesick.

Just like I am today. Amazingly, these forty years later, the taste in my mouth is the same. The feeling in my stomach identical. Yuck. Blah. Ugh. I think I may be getting sick.

I am not sleeping well. My diet is different. I've not been out much in this last week, in part due to bad weather, in part due to fatigue. I think I may be getting sick.

I've felt this one other time in my life. In September 2001, I went to Germany to visit a friend. I was in downtown Heidelberg when the twin towers fell in New York. Though I made it home three weeks later as planned, I felt sick the whole time. Yuck. Blah. Ugh. The same taste in my mouth and the same ache in my stomach. I thought I might be getting sick.

Homesickness always surprises me. I love to travel. Oddly, I've never had such symptoms when we've moved from city to city. Or on family vacations. Surely there's at least as much strangeness and exhaustion moving from Texas to Seattle or to the Virgin Islands? What is it about taking my things and my family along that avoids these deep feelings of being unsettled?

Homesickness is hard for me to "own." It feels like a weakness, a function of immaturity, a place of softness that makes me uncomfortable, a personal liability I'd rather deny.

I don't know. All this gives me a headache and I'm not feeling too well. I think I'll take a nap. Really, I think I may be getting sick.

▶ How do you experience feelings of being unsettled? Have you been home-sick for a place or a life circumstance that is not and may never be the same again?

God, do you heal homesickness, too?

❧ Small steps

My prayer companion is beginning to have a decided effect on my life.

I didn't until I recently realized how much I actually do pray for my children. I've become more aware of my prayers for them because when my thoughts head in that direction, a little bell goes off in my head reminding me of my prayer companion:

Almighty God, we entrust all who are dear to us to Thy never-failing care and love, for this life and the life to come, knowing that thou art doing for them better things than we can desire or pray for; through Jesus Christ our Lord. Amen.

Now, I would be lying if I said that I quote it by heart each time because I don't; but I end my prayers with that thought, the assumption that the One hearing my prayer wants and does even better things for my children than I could possibly desire or accomplish.

Now, that's a very comforting thought, especially for a mom who will be an "empty nester" in a few short months. Our youngest finally decided on a college. As I was looking at the calendar of each child's school, I discovered that they will all be gone in a single weekend. Betsy reports August 20, Jenna on August 21, and Bob begins law school again on August 22. Poof!

I sense that my prayer companion is leading me by small steps in a very good direction. There's something about actively entrusting my children to God in the context of reminding myself that God wants *more* for my kids then I could want or do. Somehow that thought fills that empty place in my heart, at least in part, with love and hope and rest and faith.

Though both my mind and my gut tell me that bigger change is coming, for now I am celebrating the real change and the real grace I have discovered in these small steps.

▶ What small or large steps of growth and faith do you see happening in your life?

God, you have heard my cry for help! Thank you, O, thank you.

Get a life

It was almost five years ago that Bob first went off to college. Throughout his four years in Austin, we heard many stories about his various friends. Sadly, we seldom had the occasion to meet many of them. With Austin being a much livelier place than Beaumont, they seldom came to visit.

In these last few weeks, Bob has had several of those friends come to visit him in Boston. And it has been a true delight to meet them. He chose so well.

As you might expect, Bob has been very busy showing these folks the city. Though I could have elected to be included in some of these ventures, I have opted out, practicing my requested "disinterested" stance.

And I've been alone a lot. It is an odd set of circumstances that while I am celebrating really for the first time what a wonderful relational life my son has made for himself, I am separated from my own. Not totally, of course, thanks to cards, calls, e-mails, etc., but significantly.

In my solitary time, I have become acutely aware of the fact that two of our three children have made lives for themselves completely apart from me. Jenna is having experiences in Africa I cannot even begin to fathom. The odds that I will ever meet any of the people who have filled her life the last several months are slim. Like Bob, she has made a life for herself and that is a very good thing.

Now Betsy will do the same. There's something about her having made the decision about where she will go to school that has spurred me to begin to imagine this passage for her in more real terms. She, too, will get a life.

In this context, I am becoming intensely aware of how much of the core of my life my children have been. For almost twenty-four years, more than half of my life, most waking moments have revolved around them, at least in the sense of dictating my priorities if not in the sense of requiring my presence.

Yes, my children are about the business of shaping their own destinies. And with that growth and freedom, I am hearing my own invitation to get a life.

► What kind of fundamental life adjustments are afoot in your world? How do you feel about them? Are you moving toward them or away?

God, it is a good thing that you are unchanging, because life is definitely not.

Visiting an old prison

I find myself visiting an old prison today. A prison I call "avoiding the shame of neediness."

I was lonely today. And ashamed of it. When friends called, why is it that I couldn't force myself to reveal my neediness? Why is it that I did not call any one of the many phone numbers I have for people who care for me, both the many in Texas and my few new acquaintances in Boston?

Loneliness is, after all, only human. In fact, a lovely part of being human, an evidence of our connectedness. In theory.

It feels to me like a weakness.

A shameful point of vulnerability.

A flaw.

A fault.

!@#$%! this old prison.

I hate this part of who I am as a wounded woman.

This cold, aloof, superior, hard, machine-like, unbending, frightened part of my soul.

Even as I lash out at myself, I know this is not the path to healing.

Catherine would say, "Hug her. She needs your love. She's just scared and lonely."

Tears come...and so does gratitude.

I am thankful I don't live in this prison anymore.

Though I do, from time to time, find myself visiting an old prison.

- ► Have you visited any old prisons along your way? Addictions? Compulsions? Self-destructive or simply unhelpful patterns or habits?

I hear your inviting words echo in my head, God: "For freedom Christ has set us free. Stand firm, therefore, and do not submit again to a yoke of slavery." Galatians 5:1

❧ The ducks love it

I used to think that my mood connection to the weather was just a personal idiosyncrasy. But, I realized today that it's more commonplace than I thought.

We have had horrible weather for these last two weeks in Boston. The temperatures have been twenty degrees below normal for this time of year and we've only had a day and a half of sunshine. Yuck!

For the first week, I sulked inside. I was simply tired of being cold, so I refused to go out. I stewed and brooded and stubbornly raged—all, I might add, at my own expense. It sure didn't change the cloud cover.

Now, I must admit, even in my frustration, the two times we did see sun were most graciously timed. The first was late on Sunday afternoon, just in time for me to walk to church that evening. My stubbornness had robbed me of a concert earlier that afternoon: the Passion and Resurrection portions of Handel's *Messiah*. It was still raining and I refused to go. So, I know, if it had not been for the presence of the sun, I would have once again sunk deeper and deeper into my sofa of rebellion.

Somehow, after that service, my hard heart softened. The weather did not change, mind you, clouds returning by morning, but my ability to deal with it all improved.

The only other time I've seen the sun in the past two weeks was last Wednesday, a full day of it that time. That happened to be the day Carla rescued me from my four walls for a kayaking trip down the Charles River. Sheer delight.

Since then, I've noticed how much better I've been about persevering. I went to a series of free lectures at Harvard on Friday and Saturday despite forty-degree temperatures, forty-mph winds, and rain. I went to church last night in the same.

And I noticed as I walked through the park that maybe I'm not the only being on the planet experiencing all this. Even as I chafed against the wind and wet and cold, somehow I found comfort in noticing that the ducks love it.

▶ What ordinary challenges have had an extraordinary impact on you during this difficult season? Weather? Uncooperative people? Waiting in lines? Random inefficiency?

Even as I feel the ache of life that quite simply puts me over the edge, God, open my eyes to humor, within my own reactions and all around me.

✿ Bright blossoms and thunderstorms

The trees on Boston Common are now in full bloom. All but two of the many beds of tulips are packed with bright color. Many fruit tree blossoms have already come and gone, leaving miniature apples and cherries in their places.

Yet, bright blossoms are not the only things that characterize spring.

Yesterday, we had a terrible "nor'easter" blow through. The temperatures were in the forties and the wind was gusting near tropical storm force. Though you needed an umbrella outside, it would do you little good to fight with it to stay open in such a wind. After the rains, everything around was polka-dotted with pear-tree blossom petals, beaten to the ground by the wind and rain, sticking to sidewalks and cars, pansies and street signs. The scene made me laugh even through the cold, stiff wind that remained.

Spring is a beautiful season, but it is also the season of thunderstorms in the south and, as I am discovering, some pretty awful weather in Boston, too.

This past week was odd for me, as you might have gathered from the previous few vignettes. A lot of loneliness and discouragement. Interestingly, and thankfully, the struggles have not come because things aren't going well medically. Bob is amazingly well.

Spring in Boston: a season filled with bright blossoms and thunderstorms.

▶ What is going well for you at this moment? What is not?

God of bright blossoms and thunderstorms, can't you do anything simply? I was so eager for spring. I promise, I won't complain anymore.

✢ The elephant in the living room

There's been an elephant in our living room all year long.

For the most part, I've tried to ignore it, pretending, compensating, and trying not to feed it even as I arrange my whole life around it.

These last few days, it has grown so large and menacing, it has become unavoidable. I sense that this strategy of denial will simply no longer work. It's time to do something about this monster in our lives.

The monster, sad to say, is my son's anger with me. It has operated just below the surface in our relationship for quite some time (maybe even years). It isn't explosive, but it is very real nonetheless. I assumed it was a normal part of growth into adulthood, a part of natural separation, a way to make parting easier on the soul.

In recent months, I've known it was growing. For the most part, I've dismissed it as misdirected tumor rage. And perhaps it is.

However it got there, I am unsure what exactly it is that each of us does to feed this monster. Perhaps, this living alone together without the usual buffers in place has been an elephant feeding frenzy. I hate this new growth.

In fact, it kept me up most of the night last night. And, early this morning, I actually became grateful for that.

Suddenly it is clear to me that this is no way for either of us to live: him angry and me walking on eggshells. If it is tumor rage, it's time he aimed it at the tumor, not me. It is clearly his elephant, so he will be the one to determine how we deal with it. We can learn (probably with the help of a family therapist) how we are feeding it. I accept the part I've played in this process.

Or maybe he will simply need to take his elephant to another living room.

Though I do not know the outcome, I do know that today we will talk about the elephant in the living room.

▸ Are there relational issues you have put on hold in your time of crisis that would be better off addressed?

Help.

❧ Moms are people, too

I've begun to see it more as a bad habit than anything else. As moms, we often have the tendency to forget ourselves when it comes to dealing with our kids. We simply take consideration for our own well-being out of the picture of any needy moment.

While to some extent that kind of self-sacrifice defines what it means to be a mom, from the very moment of conception there are healthy limits somewhere in all this. Without some kind of restriction on our sacrifice, we inadvertently end up teaching our children to forget us.

But moms are people, too.

I realized last night, actually early this morning, about 2 AM, that I had once again fallen into this bad habit.

And in so doing, I have fostered a very unhealthy dynamic in my relationship with my son. I've allowed him to consistently vent his anger at me without asking him to deal with it.

It hurts when his rage is forever pointed in my direction.

Moms are people, too.

And he's an adult who needs to hear about my pain. Yes, an adult with a brain tumor, but an adult nonetheless.

I am friend, not foe, and want to be treated as such. And I need him to help me understand what I do that is helpful and what isn't. I am quite sure I push his buttons, but I am not a mind reader.

He is an adult, not a child, however heavy that burden might feel at the moment.

Our talk went well. He owned his anger, albeit without a clue about how to deal with it. His preference is for me just to endure until he returns to school in the fall. He thinks this will all just go away.

I stood firm. This will not be. I am tired of hurting, and spewing anger is surely not healing for him. Though I do not know how things will change, things will change because moms are people, too.

▶ Have you sacrificed to an unhealthy degree in any of your relationships? What would it take to restore some sanity and health?

This is all so hard and so confusing. Help.

❧ Silenced

In the midst of our celebration of the end of treatment for Bob, I got news from home that has silenced me.

Within a month of Bob's initial diagnosis last August, we heard of two friends who were also diagnosed with cancer: a twenty-one-year-old woman from my parents' church and a sixty-plus-year-old neighbor.

From the beginning, their situations appeared more immediately threatening. They had both engaged much more aggressive treatment, beginning chemo and radiation very soon after diagnosis. This week I got news of both: All treatments have been discontinued. There will be no cure. The best guess is that each has only months to live.

I am so very sad for these good people and their families. I cannot fathom their grief and pain. I pray.

As you might imagine, the question surfaces: Why them and not us?

A question for which there is no answer.

I'm not even sure if I have much to say by way of discussion.

I am silenced.

Grateful.

Prayerful.

Sad. And silenced.

▶ How do you deal with those you encounter on a similar journey who have suffered less than yourself? Or more? Do you wrestle internally with either scenario?

God, sometimes life and suffering seem so random. Even when I witness your care, I feel so exposed and helpless.

❧ Some things don't average

We leave Boston tomorrow. Today is another cold and drippy day. Though I hesitated to get out in the cool, I thought to myself, "Tomorrow you will appreciate this cool weather when you hit the Texas heat."

And it's true. We are transitioning from the rainy low forties to the sunny high eighties (not to mention the ninety-five percent humidity). Too bad my weather experiences don't average themselves in any given moment. I am too cold now, and I will be too hot then.

Many things in life do average, you know. Like bathwater and bank accounts. Hot and cold, deposits and withdrawals. One extreme offsets the other. We experience the sum total, the average of sorts.

But some things don't average. Emotions don't. Life experiences don't. Seasons in nature don't. Some things don't average.

I remember the days with three preschoolers. I remember people saying to me: "Enjoy them while you can. They'll be gone before you know it."

I tried. But that was such a hard time with the constant drain on my physical and emotional stamina. Three needy voices and one tired mom. Certainly, I did enjoy my children. But I was also overwhelmed many, many days. All my attempts to logically and rationally average those days with the coming days of separation did not work.

As I find myself at the end of a life season, our nine months of tumor journey, I realize there really is a sense of ending. This will always be defined as a certain kind of experience for me: one full of both great trauma and great grace. Those facets of this time are not averaging themselves together to form some kind of ordinary life experience that will blend with the rest of my life. This has been, and will always be, a season of extremes. It is not and will not blend with ordinary life because some things don't average.

► How would you characterize this challenging life season? Do you tend to try to average that which cannot be combined in that way?

God, you have ridden every high and every low with me. Thank you. Thank you.

 # Home

What is it that makes home so wonderful?

My husband's embrace.

My children's smiles and laughter.

Trying to decide on a place to eat that pleases five opinionated people.

Gary the pug's maniac licking.

The smell of my house.

Watching Bob aggravate his sisters and telling him to stop.

My bed.

My pillow.

Walking around my garden to see what has grown and what has not.

Piling onto our bed to play Scrabble in the evening.

My well-equipped kitchen.

A grocery store where I can immediately locate random items like capers.

Evening Prayer with the monks.

Hug after hug from church members who celebrate the end of this journey with us.

Hearing "I'm so glad you are home."

Dinner at our table, with our home-cooked favorites and lots of heated debate about religion and politics.

It's so very good to be home.

► Are moments of re-orientation and "home" beginning for you? If not, are there some you can anticipate?

God, it is so good to be home.

❧ Love so freely given

We've been home several days now and folks are still inquiring about our son. The interesting thing is that almost all of these people who remember to inquire about him have never met him.

I don't know if I've ever encountered love so freely given.

Their concern is sincere.

Their prayers are real.

Their love is so healing.

Often in life, we encounter love as currency: love given in exchange for other things. We love those who make us laugh. We love those who tend to our needs. We love our children, at least in part, because they make our lives rich and full of meaning. It's only human.

To extend love even to those whom you do not personally know seems beyond human. Love so freely given is God's kind of love; a love that extends over all, is in all and through all. Like the sunshine that warms us.

I feel the warmth of God every time someone asks about our son.

I hear the heartbeat of God every time I experience this precious love so freely given.

▶ Have you experienced this love so freely given? When and where? What impact has it made on your soul?

God, once again, your body, the church, is your face and your embrace for me. How I thank you for not leaving me alone in this world. How I pray for those who are.

To dare celebration

I walked up the sidewalk at church today with Betty, an older woman from our parish. She asked how Bob was doing. It was wonderful to be able to give her such a glowing report of his freedom from complications or problems. I even sensed within myself the first signs of real celebration.

Previously, when folks inquired about Bob, I would generally give our good report with a smile on my face and ongoing concern in my heart. My "yes, but" alarm was going off no matter how confident I looked. *Yes, but the tumor might still swell and cause some problems any time in the next year to eighteen months. Yes, but we don't know for sure that it did anything at all except leave a small bald spot on the top of his head. The tumor might not be fixed; it will be at least another year until we know for sure.*

It's self-protection, really. I'm just trying to lower the velocity of this roller coaster I've been riding for the last year, make this high a little less high to avoid some dreaded stomach-churning free fall sensation in case there's another big plunging dip around the next bend.

Now, I have been giving thanks all along, but celebration is a different thing altogether. It requires a freedom of heart, a joy, a release of anxiety, and a moving away from guardedness that I have not often dared. Today the good news I spoke settled a little deeper in my soul.

Bob told me the other day, "I've done what I can and I'm moving forward with my life."

I'm trying to get there. As more and more time passes without incident, it's becoming easier. The smile on my face is slowly sinking into my heart. Ever so slowly I am beginning to dare celebration.

▶ Have you had moments of celebration yet? With or without the "yes, but"?

God, I want to trust. I want to celebrate. Make my faith and confidence in your goodness more real than my lingering fear. I want a heart that is free.

My companions on the way

Having been home just over two weeks now, I sense that it is time to draw this saga to an end. The ideas and inspiration for new vignettes is running dry.

I've known somehow from the start that this piece would end at an odd kind of unfinished place. I will not tie up Bob's treatment with a neat bow for you, my friend, because I cannot do so for myself. It will be months and months before we know if the treatment was effective and years and years before we fully discern any long-term side effects.

But before I leave you, I sense the need to express my gratitude for how you've helped me on my way.

Thank you.

I have imagined you, my faithful friends, to be patient, kind, non-judgmental, and hurting enough yourself to be tolerant of my pain.

You have listened well and been so very gentle with my ranting.

Thank you.

You have wept with me and even forgiven me when I have distanced you, at times preferring preachy theory to honest vulnerability.

You have listened compassionately to my experience even when your own was much, much more tragic.

You have understood my limitations—those things I simply couldn't write.

Thank you. You have helped me immensely.

Knowing you were there drew me toward greater self-awareness, a healing part of this journey for me. As I put my experiences into words for you, I faced them more honestly myself.

I've always believed in the power of listening. I just didn't know it could be so effective when those tuning their ears to my story are my imagined listeners.

Thank you for being my companions on the way.

God, bless these, my companions on the way, with strength and grace, comfort, and healing. Amen.

Epilogue

It has now been just more than five years since our tumor journey began. I am deeply grateful to be able to tell you that our son is doing well. Each check-up has shown the tumor to be diminishing or stable. With only a few "hiccups" along the way, his road to healing continues. Having successfully completed law school and passed the bar, he is now working as an attorney in Austin. Thanks be to God!

In my own life, over these few years, I have often pondered what impact the tumor journey has had on my soul. Though I have words for only a small part of my experience, I sense that I am much more likely to expect provision and care than ever before, in hard times and in not-so-hard times. That new faith and confidence in the love of God enabled our somewhat risky and visionary midlife move to Austin a few years ago. It is also the ground of my recent decision to continue with spiritual direction and writing rather than opting for a career path that might offer more abundant or predictable income. As we journey on together, my sincere hope for myself, my family, and you, my friends, is that more and more, we will trust the sacred healing rhythms God has written into our souls. In good times and hard times, may we live firmly rooted within the Love that embraces us all.